The
SOUL
TRUTH

The
SOUL
TRUTH

A Guide to Inner Peace

Sheila and Marcus Gillette

THE TEACHINGS OF THEO

THEO
PRESS

The Theo Group Inc. P.O. Box 90274 Palos Verdes Peninsula, CA

Library of Congress Cataloging-in-Publication Data Gillette, Sheila.
The soul truth: a guide to inner peace/Sheila and Marcus Gillette, p. cm.
Includes index.
ISBN 978- 0692646595
1. Spirit writings.   2. Archangels—Miscellanea.   I. Gillette, Marcus.   II.
Title.
BF1290.G55   2008   2008039068
133.9'3—dc22

Printed in the United States of America 1   3   5   7   9   10   8   6   4   2

While the authors have made every effort to provide accurate telephone numbers and Internet addresses at the time of publication, neither the publisher nor the authors assume any responsibility for errors, or for changes that occur after publication. Further, the publisher does not have any control over and does not assume any responsibility for author or third-party websites or their content.

Neither the publisher nor the authors are engaged in rendering professional advice or services to the individual reader. The ideas, procedures, and suggestions contained in this book are not intended as a substitute for consulting with a physician. All matters regarding your health require medical supervision. Neither the authors nor the publisher shall be liable or responsible for any loss or damage allegedly arising from any information or suggestion in this book.

In dedication
To THEO for their timeless and ever-present wisdom

Contents

Contents

Introduction

Will historians look back on the first twelve years of the third millennium as the most transformative time in the history of humanity on the planet, a time that catalyzed one thousand years of peace?

Could it be that the "spiritual age," the "new age," the "Aquarian age," the "age of enlightenment," "the shift of the ages," this new millennium really is a time of miracles and magic? A time of Spirit?

Are human beings beginning to recognize the true self as more than the physical body? As eternal spiritual beings? As a soul with full conscious awareness that survives physical death? Are we living in a time of accelerated remembrance of who we really are?

Do we have such love and compassion for humanity and the planet that each of us chose to be present now in physical form to serve this transformation in some unique way? To be living with a divinely cocreated purpose? To assist one another as we awaken to the miraculous possibilities that have been prophesied for millennia?

Are we becoming so empowered that we can manifest all of our dreams and desires simply with thought, intent, and feeling? Are our prayers capable of assisting the healing of ourselves and others?

Are we realizing the capacity to explore at will, and in full consciousness, higher spiritual dimensions and nonphysical realities by leaving our physical bodies? Are the millions of ordinary people who have extraordinary experiences of a multisensory, multidimensional nature telling the truth?

Are we now capable of developing our psychic abilities so fully that we can create real magic? Do angelic beings, or other nonphysical entities, actually speak through a human body to teach and to mentor humanity?

Will we be able to increase our life expectancy while maintaining healthy, vibrant, fully functioning bodies? And when the physical body no longer works, can we eliminate the physical and emotional pain associated with death and dying by making a conscious decision to leave the body peacefully one last time and simply never return to it after saying our final farewells?

Is it really a time of being able to maintain perpetual states of bliss, ecstasy, fulfillment, peace, full-heartedness, illumination, knowing, God-connectedness, wholeness, and totality? To actually be fully soul integrated?

Are we ready to accept that the answer to these questions is yes? There is no doubt for us that that is the answer to each of these questions. We know this from our experiences and the experiences of others. We know this from listening to our souls. We know this from the teachings of hope and possibility that the twelve Archangels are now sharing with humanity.

We encourage you only to consider the possibility that for you the answer to some or all of these questions might be yes.

We sense an unprecedented optimism, excitement, and confusion in this intensely transformational time as people all over the world are heeding the wake-up call from deep within their hearts to participate in this dramatic shift of consciousness.

Marcus: Guiding us through this mass awakening are twelve Archangels collectively known as THEO. They introduce themselves as direct messengers of God, mentors for the human experience, and the expansion of consciousness. My wife, Sheila, a world-renowned spiritual medium, has been the direct voice channel for the twelve Archangels since 1976.

Sheila: My journey began after a near-death experience in 1969. I had a pulmonary embolus after the birth of my third child. Pulmonary embolisms are blood clots that move through your bloodstream, through your heart, into your lungs. The clots block the vessels in your lungs and they burst, causing you to drown in your own blood.

We often hear about near-death experiences, but I am sure I had a miraculous healing. I was in intensive care, lying in the bed in the cubicle, knowing that if I closed my eyes I would never open them again.

I was rigid, hanging on to life and feeling as if I had an elephant sitting on top of my chest. I remember thinking, "Please, God, please, God, let me live." I had a new infant child and two small children at home, so I kept saying, "I'm the best mom to these kids. Please give me a job, I'll do anything." All of a sudden the room became illuminated with a very bright light that was just like looking at the sun, so bright I had to blink back the tears. I saw movement at the end of my bed and was amazed to see Jesus standing there. I was mesmerized by his eyes and kind face and remember thinking, "His hair is shorter and dark auburn, his eyes are hazel not blue, very different from the pictures I saw when I was a kid!" I kept blinking my eyes, but the vision was still there.

His eyes pierced me with kindness and I remember hearing, telepathically, the words, "Remember my child, you are loved." I then felt as if the top of my head had opened up. I felt as if warm honey had been poured in, seeping down through the interior of my body. My lungs were full of fluid and I couldn't breathe, but as this warmth ran down through my body I felt as if I could take a deep breath and began to relax. I now know that what I experienced was a miraculous healing. I was no longer fearful of my death.

This healing experience occurred as my family was being prepared for my death. The experience seemed timeless. It could have been hours but probably lasted only moments, and still remains as vivid today as it did when it happened in 1969.

When I got home from the hospital and my body was strong again, I started having all kinds of psychic phenomena happening to me, through me, and around me. Messages were given about other people's lives that I could not have known myself. I received information about Watergate two years before it was fully revealed. Confirmations would come almost immediately. God knew that I needed confirmation to be able to trust and continue.

It was scary when this psychic phenomena began happening to me, because I didn't know anybody who was having similar experiences, or even talking about anything like this.

After an intense two weeks of experiencing psychic phenomena, I tranced spontaneously. I began direct voice mediumship, direct voice channeling. A teacher by the name of Orlos was the first angelic being that spoke through me. He kept telling me for three years that my body was being prepared on a cellular vibrational level to be able to receive higher teachers to do the work that I had chosen, and had been chosen, to do.

One day I went into the trance state to allow Orlos to answer questions for a client and he said, "It is time for me to leave now, the higher teachers are here." I was deeply saddened by Orlos's leaving; he was my friend and my mentor who had supported me through these extraordinary experiences.

Then THEO came in very loud, very direct, and with much greater information to be shared with the world. They introduced themselves as twelve Archangels to be known collectively as THEO, not as one personality.

I was told that, among other things, I would publish a book, which I did. *The Fifth Dimension: Channels to a New Reality* was published in 1988. In this first book I wrote about my near-death experience and my psychic opening in greater detail. Now it is our time to share THEO's information in this new book of THEO's wisdom.

Marcus: The first memory I have of a personal spiritual journey was at the age of fourteen when I began having rather bizarre experiences while laying in bed at night. I would enter into a state that I know now is called "night paralysis," a state in which I would be unable to move my body and would feel completely paralyzed. These experiences were just a little bit frightening and confusing for a fourteen-year-old Catholic kid. I had no idea what was happening to me. Typically, it would happen several nights in a row, with one of two outcomes: I would either be able to utilize my free will and move myself through it and finally sit up and get out of bed, or I would find myself leaving my body and would be able to "see" my physical body lying on the bed. I would always end up safely back in my body.

Although I was very frightened by these experiences at the time, I learned that the "night paralysis" was an "arcing up" of my vibrational frequency to a point where my physical body was being protected as my Soul, or astral body, was actually leaving the physical. It became, in fact, comforting to know that we are more than our physical bodies.

As I grew older, I had these experiences less often, but my curiosity led me to research altered and higher states of consciousness. I was determined to get some answers regarding what had begun happening to me as a teenager.

Following a disappointing business venture and a divorce, lessons that were catalysts for my own personal growth, I found myself more focused on my spiritual path. I began reading everything I could get my hands on about the afterlife and near-death experiences, out-of-body experiences, psychic phenomena, and all kinds of spiritual teachings, including some channeled material.

Several years later I met a woman in a grocery store who became a close friend and who eventually gave me a copy of a book that was written by a friend of hers from Santa Fe, New Mexico, who happened to be Sheila. The book was *The Fifth Dimension: Channels to a New Reality.* I found the information fascinating.

Not long thereafter, I went to the Monroe Institute in Virginia, founded by Robert Monroe, the out-of-body researcher and pioneer. There I had a chance to experience out-of-body, higher consciousness, and multidimensional states.

I was beginning to get some answers and was experiencing other states of consciousness. In fact, I had several multidimensional experiences leading to my first meeting with Sheila. After learning that Sheila was coming to Phoenix, I asked my friend from the grocery store if it would be possible to meet her prior to the channeling session I planned to attend.

Sheila: Friends picked me up at the airport and we went to the Phoenician Hotel to meet. Marcus was the last one to join the group that evening.

I was talking with my friends when I felt an energy surge through my body. I had no idea what it was. I started looking around to see what was happening. I have had many phenomenal experiences, so when I feel an unusual energy I start looking to see where the charge is coming from. I didn't say anything to the group at the table, and a few minutes later my friend looked up and said, "Hi, Marcus." Marcus was standing at the table and I felt as if a bolt of lightning had gone through my body. It was not your usual attraction to an attractive man. It was more than that; it felt like an electrical jolt.

I knew this was an important moment, for Marcus took my breath away when I looked at him and I could not speak. I was aware that he had read my book and therefore knew more about me than I knew about him, so I said, "Well, what's your story?" When he began to talk I fell totally and completely in love with him.

Marcus: Prior to meeting Sheila, I knew that I was going to be involved in the spirituality or higher consciousness business. I had met with the Monroe Institute business manager to explore the possibility of setting up a facility in Phoenix. But I did not know at the time what was in store for me. After meeting and falling in love with each other, our purpose for coming together became very clear to both of us.

A part of our purpose is creating the Soul Truth program with THEO. The information is given to assist humanity in the spiritual and planetary transformation that we are all experiencing.

THEO's teachings speak to the dawning of the new millennium as a time of shift into a spiritual age, a dramatic shift into an age of spiritual awareness, and of the recognition of our magnificent human potential.

We've all heard talk about enlightenment, but what does it mean? We believe that enlightenment is the full soul integration that we are experiencing. Enlightenment is being light of heart, being comfortable in our bodies, being at peace, and being happy. Our consciousness is expanding rapidly now. We are perceiving more from the heart to the head, not the head to the heart. That is what is required of us now. We are here to share our experiences and to share THEO's information about how to perceive and integrate our souls fully.

We encourage you to read very carefully the information on soul integration, as the principles and tools shared within this chapter pertain to many of the other topics discussed. They will assist you in embracing the growth opportunities that are now available to everyone, for every soul manifests perfectly the experiences that are necessary for its highest learning.

This integrating of the fragmented aspects of our souls is a multidimensional, spiritual process. It is an internal, reflective, and contemplative experience that opens the pathways to one's true self, the highest self. As we become fully soul integrated, the lack of respect with which we have treated ourselves, our planet, and our fellow human beings is replaced with an attitude of love, respect, and compassion that is now necessary for our survival.

The old patterns no longer work; we are witnessing this. Throughout the world, political structures are changing dramatically and old ways of being are dissolving in our personal lives. Old patterns that have been passed along in our families for hundreds of years no longer work. We are developing new patterns of self-acceptance, of personal responsibility, of understanding on a deep level that we are here to share with one another and to have a common unity (community).

On a soul level, we have incarnated by choice; our learning in this human experience is that of emotions. The soul learns perfectly what it needs from every experience that we have in our life. There are no accidents or coincidences, no missed opportunities. In fact, every experience can be perceived as that perfect learning from which we can then move into a higher place of knowing.

We propose here a way of becoming centered in self, but not being self-centered, and practicing kindness, compassion, and being nonjudgmental with all people. This centeredness in soul then creates a more positive energetic or vibrational frequency.

Being the victim and attaching energy to old wounds no longer works. As Jesus said: "Love thyself, then love thy neighbor as thyself." We have to take care of ourselves, physically, emotionally, and spiritually. The greatest challenge that we face is to love our self, to feel worthy, and to be able to receive and accept all that we can be.

Our soul is the essence of who we are. It is energy and consciousness. Each one has a unique vibrational frequency. Many of us are now experiencing connections with people on levels deeper than we have known before, as some of the old relationships that we've held dear are no longer working for us. This can be one of the most challenging aspects of our time. As we honor boundaries and practice discernment, it will be difficult to maintain relationships with people who refuse to take responsibility for their own emotional growth, continuing to blame others for their life circumstances.

There is also recognition that we are not responsible for another's emotional maturity. It is easier to do someone else's emotional work than it is our own. It is now time to take responsibility for our own emotional maturity and integrate on a soul level.

In doing this soul work we will understand how to manifest, for our thoughts are the creative force. When we change our pattern of thought and integrate our souls, we can create all positive expressions in our life. The key is to realize that one is worthy. When we deal with life from the self, the soul, we remember the uniqueness, the beauty, and the divinity that we are.

Through daily meditation we can acquire the understanding that allows us to tap into the guidance available from the spiritual dimensions. It allows us to review the source of our fears that create agitation physically and emotionally, and to transmute those fears. All emotions derive from either love or fear. The soul integration process allows us to understand and integrate the fear, or the experience that is at the core of our patterning, that creates the agitation. As we clear these energetic blockages, we are then capable of increasing the flow of energy through our body, raising our vibrational frequency to a level much more conducive to manifesting all of our desires.

Jesus also told us "All that I have done you can do and more." We have the ability now through our thinking, our believing, and our feeling to manifest anything we desire. We can create excellent relationships, financial abundance, and physical health. Many people have limited themselves by perceiving only with their five senses in a three-dimensional body. THEO teaches us that we are not limited to the third-dimensional realities any longer. We have moved beyond even the fourth dimension, which was the recognition of ourselves as spiritual beings, into the fifth dimension, which is the expression of our true spirituality and the cognition of our magnificent powers.

There is an old Sufi saying that "only a fool believes another's word over his own experience." Many people who meditate on a daily basis are having peak spiritual experiences of ecstasy and transcendence that nourish the soul.

We are living in the most miraculous time in the history of this planet. There are many expressions of these miracles that people are sharing with us. We are creating a forum through which people can share their experiences. In our interactive public gatherings with

THEO, we hear remarkable stories from people of all walks of life. They share experiences with us that heretofore would have gone unspoken for the fear of being thought crazy.

The energy shift taking place on the planet now is activating emotions; it may be highly agitating for those who choose to resist it. There are many souls taking themselves off the planet now, who energetically have chosen not to participate in the new spiritual energy. Those who are in sync with it, who are in the flow, so to speak, are going to have experiences and recognize abilities beyond anything they ever thought imaginable. As we believe that these experiences are possible, they will be manifested.

Our personal experiences include collapses of time and space, out-of-body journeys, prophetic dreams and visions, miraculous healings, extraordinary synchronicities, confirmations of divine guidance, angel visitations, and other multidimensional adventures. It has been our experience that our souls will manifest these mystical and magical opportunities as our conscious minds place the intent. In the asking it most certainly will be brought unto us, and as each experience becomes a building block for the next, we will find it impossible to perceive only with our five senses. We intend to share more of these accounts in much greater detail in our public THEO gatherings as well as in subsequent books and CDs.

The comments that we receive from clients who have worked with THEO over the years have proven what a profound teacher THEO is. THEO opens people up to their hearts and souls. One client commented, "It is impossible not to be touched when you are speaking to angels." When people are having a personal experience with angels it opens them to a vulnerability in their hearts that they have never felt before.

People who have worked with THEO are beginning to utilize these tools to have expanded consciousness and greater fulfillment. We feel very much on purpose when we share experiences of our own, and they share theirs with us. We feel very blessed for the opportunity to work with and be taught by THEO.

It may be hard to believe that twelve Archangels would share the thoughts and words of God by utilizing the direct voice of a human being. However, it has been well documented since long before the time of Christ that God has communicated to humanity in myriad ways through many human prophets, mystics, sages, mediums, and oracles. And, of course, the thousands of confirmations experienced by those who have spoken directly with THEO have left no doubt for us of the authenticity of the source. As THEO has said, "Would a father not want to communicate with his children?"

We encourage you to take the words given forth in this dialogue into your heart and feel if they resonate as the truth for you. We are honored and proud to share with you a truly remarkable dialogue with the twelve Archangels known as THEO.

Chapter 1

Introduction to Theo

"It is the beginning, is it not?"
—THEO

S*heila:* In preparation for THEO to speak, I sit erect in a chair with my feet on the floor; I close my eyes and rest my arms comfortably on the arms of the chair, palms up.

I say a prayer of gratitude and protection and ask that information for the highest good be brought forth. I ask for God's assistance and THEO's presence.

I begin to breathe deeply, exhaling completely, for that allows me to relax, let go, move over. Then THEO enters my body on the right side of my neck and my right ear. My head feels full and my neck feels rigid. The feeling then spreads through the rest of my upper body and as they begin to speak, the rigidity spreads into the lower body. I continue to breathe as my body becomes more relaxed with this powerful energy, for at first it feels like sticking my finger into an electrical socket. There is a continual surge of high energy throughout my body while THEO is present. They always begin each dialogue with the words: "It is the beginning, is it not?"

I am aware of THEO's words while they are speaking, but after a short time I do not recall everything. If I listen to a tape recording later there is recollection.

When THEO is complete with their dialogue, this high electrical energy leaves. I open my eyes and feel a little disconnected for a few seconds. I breathe deeply to center myself again and become fully aware of my surroundings.

THEO: It is the beginning, is it not?

Marcus: **Welcome, THEO.**

We are appreciative of the opportunity to be of service unto you.

We are very pleased to have you here. I would like to start off the questioning by asking you to please introduce yourselves.

THEO is a collective group not known as one personality, but as twelve Archangelic beings that are here in this experience to share and to teach, mentors for the human experience and the expansion of consciousness.

The THEO group is not embodied but experiencing the human experience as teachers from the hierarchy of the angelic realms. We have not been fully embodied as you are. We are observers as well as teachers of a higher conscious state. We are direct messengers from the God, as one would perceive God, and we are of these angelic realms, the managers as one might think it.

From where do you speak to us?

We come, vibrationally, into the sixth dimensionary arena to communicate. However, there are twelve dimensions about the earth and we are of the higher dimensional realm. We can be in other universes, other planetary experiences, but we now teach to the earth. For there is a great shift and change energetically at this time.

There is that which is consciousness of humankind raising to a higher vibrational frequency and we are facilitators, mentors, and assistant to that.

What is your purpose for speaking through Sheila at this time?

We utilize this human body of Sheila to come forth in direct words to speak out unto humanity and to share the knowledge that is here in how to address the new patterns of being in the world, in the conscious state, being more conscious, no longer asleep to that which is the body, mind, spiritual connection and that which is the fulfillment of humankind. The recognitions of their souls are necessary and when one is fully soul recognized then they are aware that they are the spiritual being and they have chosen the experience upon the earth in a finite human body.

How did it come to be that you and Sheila have been working together for the past twenty-five years?

It was a choice of the soul to work within this medium, let us say, in this particular time to be a facilitator of this information upon the planet, engaging with these angelic beings as a teacher. It was a soul choice.

How do you merge your energies with Sheila's energy to be able to speak through her physical body?

There is a heightened frequency on a cellular level of the physical body that has been achieved by us working upon the electrical field of this body and the physicality, adjusting, as one might perceive in the adjustment of that which would be the frequency of a radio, fine-tuning, as it were, so that there could be a melding of our energies as we bring them down to a lower vibration to meet and conjoin on a cellular level so that this communiqué can happen.

So what happens to Sheila's consciousness, then, as you are speaking through her body?

There is an awareness of this soul of the information that is imparted unto the world. However, it is as if one is set aside, so that then the manipulations, let us say, of the voice can be utilized by us to communicate the words, so they can be heard by the human beings.

What is the physical impact on Sheila when you merge your energy with hers to speak through her?

There is an increased vibrational frequency. It is very electric as you might perceive it, and it does create a higher vibration on the cells so that there is then an absorption, let us say, of the hierarchy into the physical body to communicate. It is all frequencies coming together. Think in terms of magnetism. There is an attraction that is met and bonded.

Could you explain the energetic vibration that many people feel when speaking to you in person?

We do touch others in our presence and in Sheila's presence with an energetic field, for then we can address individuals cellularly so they are affected by our energetic field.

What ways are people most affected by you when in the presence of your energy field?

Many become emotional, for it allows an openness for all to recognize their totality, and it brings to the surface, on the emotional level, emotions that have been guarded, emotions that have been repressed. There is a sense or feeling of total love that then allows a vulnerability and an ability to be fully who they are, and that is quite profound. So it is, as many speak of it, heart opening.

Have you spoken through other human beings in this way before?

We have spoken to other humans, yes, not through in this way where we have been giving information directly. We have given it to them, but not through them.

So would that be to say that you have communicated to other humans telepathically?

We have communicated to human existence, yes.

And has it been in times of high transformation as we are in right now?

It is in times of high transformation or in times of great need and request.

Do you speak through anybody else other than Sheila currently on our planet?

No.

So, what differentiates your teachings from that of many spirits or entities that are speaking through human beings at this time?

Many come and speak through others, for it is in this transformational time that all of this is to happen. There are many teachers throughout the world. But that which makes this stand out is that we are not in judgment of the human experience, that we give unconditional love fully unto the beings of this planet, that we have no attachment or no agenda, let us say, or desire to control. We are here to inform, to assist when we are asked, not to usurp the free will of humankind, but be the true teachers, to lead humanity into their highest learning. There is no judgment, and there is no control.

The true teacher is one who empowers as opposed to one who usurps another's power, and that is what we have always heard in your teachings.

That is correct. We inform, we share. One is not greater than another. Each is as equal to the other. It is a sharing, you see, each being a teacher and a student. Then one says, what is it that you have to learn from us? We learn the human expression through working with you. So there is an exchange.

What else do you learn from us?

We learn emotions. We learn of the physical experience. We address and we become fully aware of the physical functioning, for we are not limited to a finite form. In essence, we see through your eyes the beauty of your world.

With so many people speaking as channels today, how do we discern what is the truth?

Each personality has an ability to discern truth. Be attentive to what the body speaks to you. The body speaks your truth. There is an awareness in the solar plexus to that which is truth. There is that which is an electrical experience in the physical body that shoots vibration, shoots a frequency when one is spoken truth to. So there is, in the physical form, the ability to know truth. To take that which is one truth and let the rest drop away, that is the discerning point.

How can we tap into the knowing or feeling that you speak of?

You already tapped into it and you already are aware of that knowing and have utilized it. It is an innate experience within the physical body of the human. It is a part of the soul as well to discern truth. One might call it intuitiveness, sensitivity. All beings utilize it. All animals have a sense of this. They would not speak of it as truth, they would speak of it as awareness, when one is safe and one is not. It is the same.

What is the best way for us to utilize your teachings to positively affect our lives?

To listen with the heart. To absorb the words but to go beyond the words to the experience. To take in the words. Not to rush about to create, but to absorb and to digest the message, and to implement that which is the skills that are given to enhance one's life experience. For those truths do come forward as tools to be utilized in the human experience, to allow one to be fully realized. So we implore humanity to listen, to take within the heart the truths that are spoken, the truths that are given, the truths that are absorbed, and to live them fully. As one lives them, and at times, seemingly illogically for some, for it is living from the heart, not the intellect. And the intellect would fight this response because it wishes control, but in allowing the heart to be in control, and to be expressed. When we speak of heart, we speak of the soul, for the soul knows fully and manifests fully what is most appropriate and for the highest good of itself.

Chapter 2

Soul Integration

*"The full conscious awareness and acceptance of all aspects of one's
soul."*
—THEO

THEO describes the soul as the whole being, the spark of creation, the spirit within, the Holy Spirit, the breath of life, that which is consciousness. It is God-centeredness, creativity. It is the frequency that allows for movement and consciousness within the physical body.

If we are more than physical bodies, perhaps even grand spiritual beings, what would it be like to fully integrate our physical being with our higher, more expansive spiritual self? At the core of THEO's teachings is that this is at hand, and the rewards of this merging of spirit and matter are magnificent beyond our wildest dreams.

It seems to us that finding inner peace and happiness is the goal of most human beings, to feel a connection within ourselves and to others in a way that makes us feel good. Maybe we even strive to have a deeper connection to that which we call God, or to our souls and possibly to find some purpose for our lives. THEO is very clear that each of us has chosen to be incarnate at this time of accelerated growth with our primary learning being that of emotions. This has been the learning for each of our souls every time we have incarnated in a human body, and we each have unique emotional patternings and experiences spanning several lifetimes.

Inherent to the soul are the memories of each experience that you have ever had in and out of the physical body. Due to the magnitude of the memories and wisdom contained therein, we seem to forget most everything upon incarnation. This lack of remembrance has also seemed necessary for us to experience our highest learning in the present lifetime. What if we can unlock these memories to discover who we really are? What if we can remember the core emotional patternings that have created the energetic blockages prohibiting us from being blissfully happy? What if we can access the wisdom of our soul to increase our vibrational frequencies to such an extent that the veils between heaven and earth, spirit and matter, no longer exist? What if we can become fully soul integrated?

Soul integration is a simple, multidimensional process that requires you to quiet the mind, center the self, and to listen, watch, and feel as your soul communicates. It is you creating short periods of time to meditate, be contemplative or reflective. Times of high emotional expression or agitation are optimum for you to go inside, to meet that fragmented aspect of your soul, of yourself, that is acting out, to have your own personal shamanic journey to the core of your being, to really begin to own your "stuff," to take full responsibility for your behavioral patternings, on your way to becoming impeccable in all of your interactions with yourself and others.

As interesting as this process will become for you, and you will have some fascinating experiences, there are reasons why it is often referred to as spiritual "work." As you remember and integrate with the perfection and divinity that you are on a soul level, you will also have to accept and be committed to changing some rather imperfect aspects of yourself on a human level. You will have to take ownership for every word, every deed, even every thought, and commit yourself to the process of spiritual growth.

Research has shown that incorporating some form of spiritual practice into your life will have a profound impact on your physical and emotional health. The majority of the world's religious and spiritual traditions recommend some form of meditation or contemplation daily.

If you are just beginning to meditate, we encourage you not to overthink it. Simply sit in a comfortable chair, close your eyes, relax, breathe deeply, exhale fully, and as thoughts enter your mind that don't serve you, just let them flow as a river into the ocean and without judgment, as you return your concentration to the breath. Soon you will look forward to meditation each day.

As soul integration is a multidimensional process, it is not limited by linear time and space, for the soul is timeless, and we can only really understand what that means by experiencing it as such. THEO's teachings, as well as our own experience, speak clearly to the eternal nature of the soul. We all have lived in human form before and will have the choice to do so again if our soul so desires. Over 70 percent of the world's population, many with religious traditions predating Christianity, believe in reincarnation. We mention this now because you may very well have the experience of integrating an aspect of your soul that was fragmented in a previous lifetime.

Our personal experience with this process of self-discovery has been fascinating and richly rewarding. We feel the light of God shining brighter than ever before into every corner of our lives. Life has accelerated at an unprecedented pace as we have become more calm and peaceful within. The time required for decision making and conflict resolution has virtually collapsed in many instances. Feelings of euphoria and deep gratitude are frequent. Daily meditation induces a lightness of being and connectedness to our souls.

You will recognize the common thread that weaves through most of the chapters in this book as Soul Integration. We encourage you to utilize the tools given here to positively affect all aspects of your life.

We have heard you say many times that we are now in a time of soul integration. Could you please explain what this means?

It is that which is a recognition of the totality of soul. What that means is that there will be a conscious understanding of the soul, of that which is the inner, higher self as many might perceive or talk about it. It is the whole being of all experiences of all time. There will be in this time to come, the new millennium, where humanity will be fully soul realized or soul integrated, meaning the ability to be familiar with multidimensional experiences or that which is of the past that has influenced the patternings of the present life incarnation. For there is the inner child work that has been done in psychological fields over this most recent past time. However, this is the step further into that recognition that there are influences, or fragmented parts of the soul that influence the patternings of one— emotional expression upon this planet. So when one integrates the incarnation present in all aspects of that, meaning the mother/father/child, then one goes beyond that expression or experience into the multidimensional expression, or the timelessness of the soul, and becomes aware of the fragmented parts of the soul that are influential as well.

What is it now about the new millennium that brings about this expression, and what is the significance of it being expressed in this way two thousand years after the time of Christ?

Know that humanity has been evolving on a physical, emotional, and psychological or spiritual level, and this is a time when the energy is present about the earth again; energy that is influenced by the world, by the outer influences or alignments of particular planets of the universe that impact energetically; and again, the two-thousand-year period, the alignment of the planets allows for this evolution of consciousness. It gives fertile ground, let us say, for the germination and awareness of one's totality, the full blossoming of the being, and a fuller awareness, not blocking in the conscious mind the past, but that which will be allowing the mind to open more fully. For the mind or the consciousness is only one-tenth utilized of that which is its capabilities, and that is all memories, all awarenesses, all vibrational frequencies. And this could become very scientific. It is not our desire to be in a scientific mode, but that which would be the teaching and the ability to share what is happening energetically to the human experience evolving now into a higher conscious state, or awareness of self.

Can you speak more to what is happening now energetically, and how that affects the soul integration process?

The energies we have just spoken about that permeate the earth's atmosphere and experiences do allow for the fertile ground, as it were, for the mind to open and to evolve, and there is a higher vibrational frequency that clears out the old patterns within the physical body, so that one is more open and receptive to the understanding of the self.

Would you describe a model for us by which a person can achieve soul integration?

That which would be the process is what we hear in this question. The process being that which would be to go within. When one is activated emotionally, is acting out from an emotional place (that is the learning upon this planet, that of emotions), it is in that time that is of one of the orphans. We speak of the fragmentation of the soul as the little orphans, aspects of personality that have been abandoned but influence how one reacts to certain stimulus in the outer world process, or experience. Relationships particularly are highly charged grounds for this acting out. However, what we speak of now, the model in that would be not unlike going within and speaking to the child of this lifetime that has been abandoned from the aspect of the present personality in an inner dialogue. The whole self, the parental self, communicates with this little child.

We take that one step beyond into the soul, which then you address, "Who inside is uncomfortable?" As you draw out these little orphans, as we call them, to communicate, there is an awareness of an age in which the abandonment occurred. There is an awareness of the circumstance in which a core pattern first began out of the need of protection and survival. With this understanding, and with this communication, as it were, there will be illumination to the mind, an awareness in the mind, of those core issues and patterns or challenges within the soul's process, and an openness of heart to bring the little orphans home. There is an emotional release when this awareness occurs to allow the emotions to surface, to be experienced, but continue the inner dialogue when one feels emotional—that is the time when there is an acting out of an orphan. This is when one can contact the orphan to become more fully realized and aware of those circumstances. When there is awareness, there is a shift of patterning, and in that shift of patterning, no longer a responding in like manners of the past to the same stimulus.

So how do we integrate and then release from being influenced by this old patterning or orphan that you speak of?

There is not release or relinquishment of this little orphan. What comes about is a recognition, an inner dialogue, the ability to know that this is where it comes from so that you need not respond in the same way again in the future. There is an awareness, no longer an unconsciousness, and when there is awareness, knowledge, then one can move forward and not react in an old pattern. Then there is a continuum of recognition of this little orphan, not a relinquishing of it, for it is a part of the self that is brought home into wholeness. The heart is open then to receive the orphan home, no longer segregating or separating from it in the sense that it is not good enough, to be loved fully. It is much like the child of this incarnation that had been abandoned, set aside, out of the belief of not being lovable enough or good enough. You encourage, you love these little orphans. That allows them peacefulness, a sense of belonging and wholeness that allows integration and the support of the self fully.

In hearing of this process people would probably say it sounds very similar to the inner-child work in psychological fields.

It is very similar to that, yes. Only it goes beyond that. It does not stop with the child of this lifetime. One does not delineate time, it becomes timeless. Because when you begin to contact the little orphans, there is a timelessness about it. Take no thought for time, for as you will see in your environment in psychological fields, there are memories that do arise for particular individuals that seemingly do not relate to this present lifetime. That is because they have tapped into the soul and its fragmentation that influence the patterns of this lifetime. They cannot delete or ignore these feelings or these remembrances, but they put them in the right place in time.

It sounds very similar to a shamantic soul retrieval journey. Can you speak to the similarities between the two?

It is very similar. In the shamanic journey or soul retrieval, however, there is the usage of the animal side of self. Meaning, that of this earth there is that animalistic property in all beings. That which would be the animal totems in your indigenous people's beliefs that refer to aspects of personality. So there are similarities to these processes. However, when we speak of that soul integration fully, we are speaking of the human experiences that have separated self.

What types of circumstances over the lifetimes that we have lived do you refer to as the moments of fragmentation?

There are different kinds of abandonment of aspects of personality out of the need of survival, much like the inner child, much like what happens in this incarnation to some who have been abused, hurt emotionally or physically. There occurs a separation at a particular age of the aspect of the personality that is deemed necessary to abandon for survival's sake. That is a fragment of the personality, just as in the inner child work of this incarnation for many, it is a fragment of the whole personality. It is a part *of.* Think in terms of the being as a diamond with many facets. It is only one facet, you see.

So you could be fully integrated with the inner child of this incarnation and yet still remain highly fragmented and agitated because you are not incorporating all of your previous lifetimes into the process?

That is correct. So it is humanity has been brought along, educationally speaking, psychologically speaking, evolving in consciousness for some time. The inner child work has been a stepping-stone for that process, just as other works psychologically, that have been done over the years, have been stepping-stones for a greater understanding of the mind and consciousness of the human. So what comes about now in your psychological teachings and realms is more that which would be transpersonal, meaning that it would incorporate not only the psychological experiences and the mind of this present time, but the expansion of spirit, mind and body. Incorporating all those aspects is important for the wholeness of the person and the healthfulness of the person. All are interrelated and should be integrated. Integration is integrity. Integrity is wholeness. Wholeness is holiness. And again, when one achieves this, there is the recognition of one's holiness, meaning the uniqueness, the beauty, the divinity that you are.

So you are suggesting that we listen and be aware of the emotional responses in our daily lives, the agitation or any experiences that create a feeling of nonpeacefulness. That these would then be the times to go within?

Yes. It is an indication in your external world, meaning your physical body, your external circumstance, that it is time, for it has been made manifest in your experience. At any time that one is agitated, uncomfortable in an emotional way, and a physical way, for it does affect the physical vibration, then it is time that there is an opportunity of exploration, of understanding, of integration. It is a time of acting out, that is charged electrically so one can have the memory, a remembrance of experience, of drawing forth an opportunity of understanding. And if it is not present in that immediate consciousness, it is to ask for it to come forward, and there will be times it would come forward in the dream state, or in a quiet mind state, or in a meditative state, whatever quiets the mind to allow it to surface.

What would be the most optimum technique that you can recommend for us to begin this process?

There are those who have this intensity who cannot do it on their own, that could utilize a facilitator or a therapist or communicator to assist them. But many can do it upon their own process who have been doing their inner work revealing unto themselves the self. That process can be a meditation with intent of understanding, and in the asking it is given, asking the self to bring it forward, a readiness for receptivity of the information, the meditative state, quieting the mind, going inside to communicate with the self. There will be those who will be visual. They will be able to see who it is, the age, the gender, the being and seeing the whole self standing next to this little orphan, letting it know that it is loved and is going with you into your new life. Those who are visual can do it in this way as a dialogue. Others are sensory perceptors and will not see but will feel the energy and can communicate through feeling. Others are auditory, they will hear the communication, or a combination of all of them. So it is a process, but be not disheartened if you are not seeing, if you are not visual, or a visionary, because whatever form is acceptable psychologically and emotionally to the self will be the modality used. One is not greater than another. Each is equal in their intensity. They are only different.

What is the goal of this process?

Peace in the heart, joyfulness in life, fulfillment of one's path, and understanding of one's learning process and purpose, all of this is for the fullness of self. The happiness of being which we have spoken of as contentment in heart, a comfortableness within one's life process, a joyfulness, ecstatic living. Total awareness. Moment to moment, day to day.

Are there any mistakes that one can make as one begins the process of achieving full soul integration?

There are no mistakes. There can be none, when the intent is for fulfillment, for wholeness, and that intention is not negated by a negative thought. For a negative thought that it cannot be done would only stop the process for a time. But there are no mistakes.

What would be the beliefs that people would hold that would block them from this process being effective for them?

Fear. Oftentimes many believe if they allow the memories to surface, they are going to find out they are as bad as they really think they are. Ultimately, it is the other side of that. They will find out that, yes, they have had experiences, human experiences for the learning process, that they have learned from, and would find that they have a goodness of heart and love far beyond that which they have allowed to receive or to be experienced. When one can come into the place of full love of self in this manner, they would be able to radiate that out into their world circumstance and manifest that love in their *life* externally, on every level. Receptivity is the key, and that is what will happen in the process: an openness to receive, fulfillment, happiness, joyfulness, connectedness. All of these things come to fruition when one allows the self to be whole.

And then what of those who say that this process sounds completely crazy? What do you mean, little fragmented aspects of my soul, who are they, where do they reside, what does this really mean? There will be those who have that reaction.

They may, yes. We can say nothing to that. For if that is their response, they have closed the door, have they not? It is a choice. If one says yes, and proceeds to implement the process, then they would have the experience and then they would understand the meaning. But if they choose not to engage in the process and to judge it from nonexperience and nonunderstanding, then they block their process.

And probably will find themselves fairly agitated with the energy that is present today, won't they?

Yes, there is great agitation with it. So it is, rather than trying to fight the river, it is to flow with it. And there are greater things to come.

How will the integration process help us answer such universal questions such as "Who am I?" "Why am I here?" and "What is my purpose?"

When one is fully in touch with their soul, then they have the answers of their being.

And how do those answers come to us? What form do they take?

First comes from an inner knowing, and then it is made manifest in the outer world experience. And if one is on the path of their soul, and fully aware of it, there is great joy, and there is flow within that. If they are going against and refusing to receive and to understand and to be aware, then they would have difficulty and angst about their path, their life, their experience, and they would feel victimized by life.

What is your definition of the soul?

The soul is that which is the whole being - the spark of creation. That which is what one might call the spirit within, or the Holy Spirit, the breath of life, but it is that which is consciousness. It is the frequency that allows for movement and incognition in the physical body. It is that God-centeredness; creativity. It is being. One could not move the physical structure, could not breathe if there was not a soul.

In my own process with the soul integration techniques that you've taught me, I found many times what appears to be a movie reel that I see in meditation with multiple faces that run through this movie. Are these, I suspect, aspects of myself from previous incarnations?

Can be. It is dependent upon that which would be the request.

Sometimes they show up with no request being made at all.

They do not request. You request them. There is a need of communication with these beings. Know that in your circumstance, it can be guidance that is about you, guides, mentors, angelic beings. It would be a discernment on one's part as there **would** be these visions. You can ask in the experience, who is it? Why are you here? So it is communicating, not assuming. Your particular way has been visual. Others will not be as visual but will be sensory. So it is not to think it is only one way.

Is there a differentiation between what people would define as enlightenment and full soul integration?

They go hand in hand. For to be fully integrated on the soul level, fully aware, masterful, as it were, of who you are, you are enlightened. For then there is the lightness of heart, the lightness of being, the wholeness of being. Both terms mean the ecstatic feeling, total awareness, the ability to know all things, and to be comfortable within that knowing. Total acceptance. We can give you all of these words. Words are very limiting. But it is that which is fulfillment of heart, joy, peace.

Will our life expectancy be expanded as we become soul integrated?

Yes.

What is our potential in this time relative to our ability to live longer, healthier lives?

One hundred and twenty years is capable. As beings become more aware and cognizant of all aspects as we've been speaking about, there is a greater healthfulness and a timelessness that can be achieved.

How do our diet and physical well-being influence soul integration?

As one becomes more fully realized, one is more cognizant of what the body needs and feeds it properly. There is not one particular diet, or one particular way for each being, for each body has its own structure, its own chemistry, it's own soul. So one would be attentive and fully aware of what the body speaks to it that it needs to maintain its full healthfulness.

Are there masters today, fully integrated souls, walking on earth?

There are.

Did they inherently know this process on a soul level prior to incarnating?

Some were integrated and came as teachers, others experienced the integrational processes and became it, others, to model....born fully aware. Not many of those.

We probably only have to look at their example to know who they are, don't we?

Correct.

When do you see the majority of the population moving into this place, and will it happen in our lifetime?

In the new millennium. It would not be in your present lifetime that this will happen for the entirety of the world. But you would see great numbers, yes. Change.

So this is really the essence of the shift into a higher state of consciousness, isn't it?

It is.

Some people speak of this shift of consciousness as an "awakening to zero point." Can you speak to that as it relates to the soul integration process?

One and the same, but there are many ways of expressing it for there is a need now for all beings to understand and to hear, so there is the need for particular vernacular or words to be given so that it can be heard.

What other forms are people speaking of it in?

As we are, in the sense of spirit. Others speak in terms of intellectual, others speak in terms of scientific. When you speak of zero point and vibrational frequencies and degrees and energies, these can all be scientifically explained by some so that there would be those minds that could grasp those particular words. For the mind sees in pictures, experiences, for its understanding. So if one is of a particular mind-set, intellectually speaking, and that is what is understood, then there would need to be words given to that mind for an understanding of the process. For many of those types of minds would not listen to, or heed, or take in what we speak of because it would seem not as finite.

It is experiential. It is feeling. It is not intellectual. And there are those that pride themselves on their strong intellect and it would be necessary to speak to them in terms that would be acceptable, so that there is receptivity, and the ears and the mind are open to hear and not blocked by a particular word or way of speaking.

We know that we can measure vibrational frequencies and energy, but is there a measurement today to prove the existence of the soul?

No, there is not.

Is this something that will happen in the near future?

There are some scientists that would like to be able to express that they have found the energy of the soul. There are others that say it cannot be, that there is not such a thing, it cannot be measured. There are ways of measuring energy and electricity and all of these kinds of things, and there has been speaking about consciousness in a particular way, and the ability to transmit thought. There will be measures of all of these examples, but does it measure fully the soul? No.

There are people on this planet who would be perceived as self-masters, as highly successful, highly disciplined teachers. What is the relationship between self-mastery and soul integration?

Self-mastery is a mental capability, an intellectual process. It is that which is a training. Soul integration is an experience of totality. Self-mastery is that which is engaging the intellectual mind in a particular pattern, or way, to be more efficient. And not that that is not necessary, but it continues to keep the being in their head rather than in the experience of the soul or the heart. Not to say that it is not a good process. It is good training, but to go farther than that in the exploration and acceptance of one's self. To achieve totally the feeling of peace and connectedness.

After becoming fully soul integrated, is there another step in our spiritual evolution?

Living it. When one lives the fullness of the soul, then comes about that which would be peaceful expression of experience upon the earth in a full body. As one might think of living heaven on earth, a radiance of love unto others, a radiance of love unto the earth heretofore that has not been fully expressed. And all beings have that capability. It is time, it is opportunity, to express that fulfillment now.

�֎ *Reflections on Soul Integration*

Definition of soul integration
- Full recognition of the totality of the soul including all multidimensional aspects; knowing the full self beyond the physical body
- Conscious awareness, understanding, and remembrance of all experiences in the present lifetime and others that influence the emotional patternings of this incarnation
- An acceptance and integration of the fragmented aspects of the soul leading to wholeness, fulfillment, and enlightenment
- Can be thought of as multidimensional inner-child work

The planetary energy of the new millennium creates this opportunity for accelerated growth
- Humanity has been evolving to this point.
- The planetary alignments two thousand years after Christ create optimum energetics for evolution of consciousness.
- The time is now fertile to access the 90 percent of our consciousness that has not been utilized.
- With an increase in vibrational frequency, the old patterns can now be cleared out of the physical body.

A model for achieving Soul Integration
- When you become agitated, or otherwise activated emotionally, it is then time to go within.
- Know that you will be acting out, or responding emotionally, because of an emotional patterning that originated with an aspect of your soul becoming fragmented in this lifetime or another. THEO refers to these fragmented aspects of your soul as "little orphans."

- The "little orphans" become detached from the total soul, the adult soul, out of the need of survival due to trauma, abuse, or some other core issue or emotionally devastating experience.
- Center the self. Quiet the mind. Close your eyes and relax. Breathe. Exhale fully.
- Begin an inner dialogue with yourself. Ask who inside of you is uncomfortable. Be patient.
- Visually, auditorily, or sensorily you will begin to experience this aspect of yourself, communicating to you.
- You may become aware of an age, gender, or, at the very least, a circumstance (core issue) in which the separation or abandonment occurred.
- Illumination regarding the core circumstance will eventually occur in the asking if you are patient. It may not happen in the first meditation. It may occur in another meditation, in full waking consciousness, or in the dream state.
- Allow for an emotional release when this awareness occurs. Allow the emotions to surface, to be experienced fully. Do not ignore or repress them.
- Communicate with this aspect of yourself (little orphan) and open your heart to hear and to feel, and to welcome him or her "home" to return and to integrate with the adult or full soul.
- Let this recovered aspect of your soul know that you love it unconditionally and you welcome it fully into the whole soul as you take it with you into your new life.
- You will emotionally, energetically, and even physically feel the awareness present.
- With this awareness comes a shift in patterning.
- With this shift of patterning, you will not respond in like manners to the same stimulus.

Benefits of Soul Integration
- A cleansing of blocked energy will result in an increase in your vibrational frequency You will feel more lighthearted, more fulfilled.
- You will experience greater peacefulness, a lightness of being.
- You take full responsibility for your emotional growth.
- You become empowered, for you will know the source of your emotional patternings.
- You will cease to blame others for your life circumstances.
- You may begin to recognize the journey of spiritual self-discovery as the grand adventure that it is.
- You forgive yourself and eliminate the fear associated with thinking that you were going to find out that you are as bad as you thought you were.
- A full remembrance of all the wisdom and experiences known by your whole soul, your highest self.
- Bliss, ecstasy, and enlightenment moment to moment; truly living heaven on earth.

Additional thoughts on Soul Integration
- There are no mistakes.
- With intent, commitment, and awareness of the process, you will succeed.
- Those who choose not to acknowledge the source of their emotional patternings will feel great agitation.
- Your life expectancy will increase, for you will become more aware of the needs of your body.
- Self-mastery is a mental capability and an intellectual process that is learned in the mind. Soul Integration is an experience of totality, an experience of the soul and of the heart.
- A transpersonal therapist or facilitator can be of assistance if you feel the need.

Chapter 3

Relationships

"Old patterns no longer serve humanity. New relationships are being formed from preference, not need, as the relationship unto the self is most important."
—THEO

Is there an area of our lives more affected by the current planetary energy shift than that of relationships? Every aspect of our lives seems to be up for review, as we recognize the old patterns that no longer work for us and wait for the new to be formed. Most people are experiencing numerous opportunities for growth and change, as this heightened energetic frequency is responsible for the activation of emotions unlike those which we have experienced before. It really makes us take a look at our "stuff." Attempting to resist opportunities for emotional and spiritual growth will lead to further agitation for, as THEO says, "That which you resist will certainly persist." Embracing the growth opportunities inherent to relationships can propel you to a heightened level of fulfillment and connectedness with your primary partner and in all other relationships.

Relationship patterns that include that giving away of your power, or your looking to another to make yourself whole or fulfilled, no longer work. Relationships based on new thought are those that are formed from preference, not need. Having a loving relationship with yourself, becoming fully soul integrated, allows you to manifest relationships of equality and empowerment. Now, more than ever, the self-defeating patterns, that, in the past, created unhappiness, are unnecessary.

Recognizing that the soul manifests perfectly what is necessary for its highest learning, you can see how each relationship mirrors that which is most appropriate for your growth. Many people are now realizing that they do not have to be engaged in the cycles of patterns associated with past failed relationships. In this time of increased awareness, you can discover the patterns that have created a lack of love and fulfillment and how they have contributed to your fear of being hurt and of repeating mistakes.

Spiritual relationships are now being formed. These new relationships nourish the soul as each partner is fully supportive of the other's spiritual growth. A sense of purposefulness is evident in these relationships, a desire to make a difference in the world, to be of assistance in some way to humanity, together. There is a full honoring of the other's path, whatever it might be, for neither sits in judgment of the other. Couples in these highly evolved relationships meditate together regularly and integrate spirituality and sexuality in the tantric practices of the East, bringing about a profound connectedness to the other and to the Source of creation. We recommend these practices to couples wishing to achieve expanded levels of consciousness together. And you will enjoy the best sex you have ever had.

In the following discussion, THEO proposes the use of several books that you may use to create new patterns that will serve you and benefit your life process.

You have said many times that we've taken physical form as spiritual beings to learn emotions which would be most often learned through our relationships with others. You have also stated that you learned of emotions through us. Please explain.

We learned that which is emotions through the human experience. As to relationships that we see here, it is important to the well-being of humanity that there is relating on a basis of new thoughts. Being that which would be the evolution of consciousness at hand allows relationships to come more fully into balance on an emotional level.

Can you explain to us what a soul mate is?

Soul mate is more than one. One can perceive it as that which is soul family as well. It is entities that are embodied, or not embodied, that are supportive on the same wavelength, same soul age, have a knowingness, and incarnate together, time and time again to support one another's growth. There is an equality, there is a nonjudgment, there is an acceptance. But most important that which is of the soul family is that which is a vibrational frequency or alignment from one's soul to another on the same level. It is also that these are groupings, family of souls or soul mates, as it were, that do come together for specific purposes in which to share and support the growth.

This would also include those that evoke negative emotions in us as well.

Oftentimes those that are most difficult, let us say, or challenging, can be that which is the highest teacher. One oftentimes perceives soul mate in a romantic sense but it does not mean because one is a mate of soul or that of the soul family it would be an easy relationship. For at times they could be greatly challenging, for that is the commitment for the expansion and growth of the individuals.

Do soul mates come in and out of our lives for short periods of time and are then not to be seen again in this lifetime?

They will continue, but not necessarily in the present lifetime, but in the sense of connectedness, yes. Soul mate or soul family connections are eternal.

How do we know for sure when we have met a soul mate?

When one perceives the numbers of individuals that are truly attracted in one's life experience, they number very few. There is a recognition on a soul level of knowingness. And attraction: if there would not be a connection there would not be an attraction, whether it be positive or negative; a response. However, in that which is soul family the attraction is strong and most often positive.

We have romanticized the concept of soul mates and established it as a goal for ourselves romantically. There is also a twin flame or a twin soul that is said to be the deepest connection possible. Can you explain?

That which is a twin flame is the partner or the other aspect of the same soul. Meaning, it is the male/female, positive/negative, yin/yang, whatever one wishes to comment upon in the verbiage. But that which would be a twin flame is the masculine and feminine of the soul. One being fully embracing the masculine and the other feminine. On coming together, there is recognition. There is a recognition of likeness, of attunement energetically, a sense of oneness, physically as well as emotionally and spiritually. There is no doubt.

What happens between two people who are twin flames when they come together? What are some of the physical manifestations of that soul level connection?

Complete attunement. A sensitivity and a sense of empathy physically. Feeling, thinking, experiencing. It is a physical vibration that is felt in the bodies. It is a high-pitched physical vibration that can be sensed. There is a feeling of when one has a pain the other feels it. So there is a complete alignment energetically. And there is that which is an understanding and a fullness of being in connectedness to heart.

Sheila and I have had experiences of this nature, whereby we will be thinking of each other, and be a thousand miles apart, and have a vibrational or electrical experience and know that we are being thought of at that moment. Is that common with twin-flame relationships?

Yes. Now others would speak of this as well, but they would not be the greatest of intensity as this is felt between their twin. Do you understand?

I do. But if we in fact possess a single soul within these human bodies, it begs the question regarding the confusion of being of the same soul in two separate bodies. Can you explain?

There is that which is the soul, that is the masculine side and the feminine side, not always are they incarnate. But they are constantly connected. So that when one does express the masculine and feminine of the totality, it is that which is a balance of both expressions, an awareness, an integration.

Does each person have a twin flame, whether or not it is incarnate in a physical body?

Yes.

Every soul is part of the half whether it be the male or the female?

Yes.

Would it be true that in a twin-flame relationship, for instance, the male half would always be embodied as the male and the female would always be embodied as the female?

Each would have an experience at different times of male and female, but when both are embodied, one would be fully that essence of who they are. Meaning the feminine being feminine and the masculine being masculine, whichever is that true essence or aspect of the soul.

What more can you tell us about soul mates of twin souls?

It is not to be enamored by this perception. It is to come together in relationships and to be fully present within them, in that environment of what one manifests in one's experience. For the soul, and one must trust this, manifests perfectly along one's path what is appropriate for the growth, for relationships, for experiences. There are no wrong choices. However, when one meets a mate of soul or family member, there is a recognition and there are agreements prior to incarnating, for these groups, together. And if one is to be embodied fully with the twin flame, there will be a meeting at a particular time of readiness for this understanding and expression.

Do we have an agreement prior to coming into these bodies regarding the relationships that we will manifest in this lifetime?

Yes. The soul has a plan.

What is the interaction between destiny and free will in choosing our relationships?

Know that the soul, if one allows a recognition of the soul and the following of the soul, which is the heart and that full awareness of one's path or choices, going with the flow, as one might perceive it, is a cocreation of the life circumstance. So if one chooses not to participate, that can be a choice, do you see, that the soul will draw into an experience other opportunities. But at a point of recognition, on a soul level, whether it is embodied or not, if one has chosen not to continue the plan, let us say, they would again assess that and make adjustments.

Does karma play into this relationship?

Yes, karma being that which is opportunities of growth, agreements, contracts of growth, and learning, one unto the other. Many think of this as a payment of debts, so to speak. It is more an opportunity to rectify particular circumstances or to learn from experiences. It's not good or bad. When one is learning in the educational system, whatever education they are learning, and the teacher places forth in front of the student an opportunity of learning, you may call it a problem, whatever it might be perceived as, that needs to be addressed, clarified, and worked through. This is no different, you see, for a greater understanding. One is given the tools through that process to shift and change perceptions, attitudes, to grow and utilize new skills and tools. So when one thinks in terms of the educational process of the soul it is no different than the education of the mind.

We are prone to allowing our intellectual minds to create obstacles out of the fear of being hurt or abused in some way as we may have been from a prior relationship. How do we transmute that fear?

Through the recognition of patterning with the being, communication within the being, to those fragmented parts of the self that influence those thoughts. The patterning of beliefs of not being good enough, or hurt, or whatever it might be, were created in a particular circumstance. So when one becomes aware of the core circumstance that created that pattern, then one resolves it from within, integrates it, acknowledges the worth of self, let us say, and the love of self, and then the pattern is transmuted into a new way of being. So there is an awareness, as one observes particular patterns in one's life, to go within and to communicate within the soul, or with the soul, to become aware and enlightened to those aspects of being, how the core issues first created the separation and belief of not being good enough began. Then as one has this self-realization, new patterns can be formed out of self-love. When a circumstance or opportunity arises that is similar or familiar to this old pattern, one perceives it differently and reacts differently and does not need to react in manners of the past, and can implement these new patterns within the being, and respond in a different manner.

In speaking of the old patterning in relationships, what is it that is no longer working for us?

The patterns that do not work any longer are patterns that are a lack of self-esteem or self-worth, patterns of passivity, meaning that which would be relinquishing one's power to another in the hope that one would fulfill the other. It is the individuals coming into wholeness to express fully who they are in an independent way, in an integrated way, into relationships. Oftentimes beings come into relationships from the wounded point of view, expecting the other personality to heal them, to take responsibility for them in some way rather than they taking responsibility for their own emotional maturity. This will no longer work. The dominance, the passive, the control over another, usurping another's process or free will, blocking another's growth—all of these patternings that have been in the past, that have been one subservient, one in control, do not work. Each being must take full responsibility for his or her own emotional maturity, his or her own life process. And as this comes to fruition, relationships will be on a much higher level, meaning that one would not blame the relationship for his or her life not working. One would take full responsibility for his or her own actions and reactions and express and communicate from the heart, not from a manipulative place of need. What forms are relationships that are preferential, not needy.

You talk about shedding the old patterns, letting go of the old wounds, moving out of the place of being the victim. These traits are very deeply embedded in many people.

Yes, it has been cyclic over and over and over again. Family to family, family member to family member, male to female, on and on for hundreds or thousands of years. And that is what is shifting and changing now. For beings are no longer unconscious to these patterns and, first and foremost, coming into a relationship within the self in integrating the wholeness of being and expressing that out into the world in all relationships. For when one is fulfilled within the self, integrated within the self, whole within the self, and if one translates the spelling of that word *whole,* Holy, then one expresses, in the relationship in the outer world, wholeness or holiness. For that then is the expression of the perfection and divinity of the soul.

Speak more to the process of transforming from a place of feeling the "victim," or the "wounded," into a place of strength and wholeness.

We have spoken a bit to this in the sense of going within, accessing the aspect of self that has been abandoned, fragmented off, separated from. One communicates on an inner level with this little orphan, as we would call it. Many call it the inner child. It is taking a step further into fragmentation of the soul, for there are different ages, different times, different genders, that one has been on a soul level that this has happened to, that do influence the patterns of life experience. When one becomes communicative inwardly with these little orphans there begins a dialogue of understanding of where it first began, the pattern or wound. There is an awareness of it and the whole self. The adult self becomes aware and is the best parent for this little orphan, letting it know that it is loved and will be taken into the new life, not set aside or abandoned, as has been in the past, and would be given a voice. It would not have to act out in these old ways.

Would meditation be the most effective way to begin this integration process?

Quieting the mind, using the breath, going within. Yes. It is a form of a meditation for the inner dialogue. For meditation quiets so one can hear.

Share with us your insights on the concept of being happy as opposed to being right.

That comes from the patterning of self-righteousness and judgment, also relinquishing one's power to another. For as one wishes to be happy, one becomes integrated to the self. For one cannot be happy with the old patternings that dictate the need to control, or to be right, or to judge another. For what comes about in the fullness of being integrated, the fullness of self-acceptance and self-love is a relinquishing of that need to control, or self-righteousness, meaning that one no longer projects out the fear. For the need to be right and to control, for that is a controlling issue, is fear based. That one would not be heard, one would not be acknowledged, one would not be loved. There is a projection of that into the world and to relationships. Happiness is what is being sought, but ultimately it is that fullness or integration of the self, the wholeness of being, that brings about a comfortableness within the heart, a love of self, a radiance of the being-the-divinity of the being shining forth.

We always have a choice in any conflict to act from a place of anger and judgment, rather than compassion and nonjudgment.

That is out of a lack of interaction with the self. To react out of anger and projection of one's pain is a lack of communication, particularly of a communication from the heart, the truth of the being, the ability of vulnerability, allowing the self to be fully open, not guarded, expressing one's full truth. And also on the other side when one communicates. Communication is necessary not only in the speaking, but in the listening, in the hearing. So make a full commitment in relationship to that communication, which is truly communication, speaking truth from the heart and maintaining the ears open to hear that truth. For oftentimes when beings begin to communicate, or try to communicate, when one speaks, another oftentimes is responding before there is a full statement made, and one is not heard completely. Then there is anger, for not fully listening is controlling as well. Relationships are best served by clear communications, speaking and listening, not from the defensive point of view, not from a blaming point of view; meaning that when one speaks to another it is well to speak of one's feelings, claiming one's own responsibility, not pointing the finger in blame, so that then the one that is listening to the statements made will remain open and nondefensive. The ears will remain open to hear and the response will be more heartfelt in one's truth, not from a stance of protection. When one feels attacked, do they not protect?

Can you speak more to the role of cause and affect in relationships?

Act and react. To every action there is an equal reaction. That is the law of your science, is it not? It is true in communicating as well. Be cognizant of one's speaking. Be cognizant of communication, clearly. What is the intent behind the words? For oftentimes, words are given and the intent is given in such a way to harm, to hurt, to wound. So clear intention of word, first of thought, and word, is extremely important. Attentiveness to communication is necessary. Think before you speak. If one is mindful of the words that are given and thoughtful of intent, then one can express clearly from the heart and not the woundedness of the being. However, when listening, it is important to be attentive as well, yes? For oftentimes a response from another that is listening to a particular comment is also colored by the patterning and the insecurities and the fears. Each party, in a conversation, must be attentive, aware. Aware of their own patterning, aware of their own issues, before responding unto one another—action, reaction. Most often, in the human expression, beings are not attentive, they are reactionary, one to the other, out of a place of unconsciousness of these patterns. What comes to fruition now, and that is what is changing for humanity, is that consciousness will be there and it shifts and changes the way beings communicate to each other. That is a blessing.

It is a blessing, and I would ask you to give us some conflict resolution guidance. How would one most effectively solve a conflict or heal wounds in a relationship?

When communicating, speaking from the feeling point of view. Speaking, "I feel…when this happens," "This is my experience …" When one speaks clearly to their own feelings, they are taking responsibility for themselves.

As opposed to "you make me feel…"

Yes. No one makes anyone anything. It all comes from within. Action and reaction. If one does an action, whatever that may be, and another perceives it in a particular way and reacts from their own being, they are not forced to react in any way. They fully implement the emotional response.

We always have a choice in terms of how we react to any situation.

Always. There is a choice. So it is to be aware, to take a moment before responding, centering in the self and recognizing one's own emotions, listen attentive, responding to one that has spoken and, first off, recognizing as they speak, "I am aware, I have heard what you have said." For most often beings become angry when they feel not heard. So when they are heard, then the energy shifts and changes, and there is not so much confrontation. When one is acknowledged, there is a feeling of acceptance. It may not be liked, but if one speaks the truth, it will always be accepted. It may not be liked. But it would be accepted if it is heard and the intent is pure. Then there can be true communication. It is necessary for all humanity, all beings, to make the commitment unto the self, to take full responsibility for their own emotions, not placing that responsibility on another, for when one does this there will always be disappointment, for another cannot fulfill the other; not to need another defining the self, for each being can only be the definer of themselves.

As we move into the spiritual age, people talk of spiritual partnering, or having relationships of purpose. How would you define this type of relationship?

Know that each partnering has purpose. It is that which is the learning of the soul that is an integration of self, the opportunity to engage with another in the depth of being, and the primary relationship being that which is of greater learning. For one mirrors unto the other what is necessary for growth. That has always been true. But now there is that which is the consciousness of the human, and of the experience of being in relationship, that does highly evolve the soul. So in that it is more purposeful for there is that which is more awareness. An understanding of one's experience being that of the expansion of the soul, being that which is eternal, being that which is not only of one lifetime but many. So it is that which would be a recognition, a fulfillment of the soul, a recognition of that which is multidimensional expressions of the soul. It is that which would be a coming together with soul family, meaning there is full recognition of the connectedness that is eternal one unto the other. There is also that which is relationship to others from other times, other places, but not of the soul family, one could think in terms of acquaintances. The soul family is that which would be the group that would live in your home, so to speak. Those which are the acquaintances, or compatible souls they may be called, are those that you might perceive as neighbors, in the neighborhood, workmates. All of these do influence, do interact. We gain and learn from each other but that which would be not as connected and not always eternal.

How do you define the male and female roles in the new millennium?

There is the expression and it is physiological as well as spiritual in the sense of male embodiment and female embodiment. The female oftentimes is that which is internal, that which is the intuitive, that which is the expression of spirit, the nurturer, the bearer of the young. The male is still that model of protector, of that which is the outer expression of the soul, meaning, that which is the warrior, the being in the world, the provider. These rules were not dictated by society, but have been dictated by physicality and necessity. That remains the same, for that essence continues to be the same. However, through this time and going into the new millennium, there is a greater awareness of each soul, and it can express more fully all aspects of being; that the male can be, and addressing to, their intuitive, that their response in a warrior-like way is intuitive just as one would be on the battlefield. The male is intuitive. What one would find is that there is greater acceptance of the speaking about it. The female, the nurturer, is as well a warrior and has been in the past. So what there would be is a blending of these skills and an acknowledgment and an empowerment from within. But you continue out of choice to express those roles and those bodies that are dictated by the physicality. There are certain physical attributes to a male in that which would be strength, in that which would be able to be in the exterior, out of physical strength, skin thicker, body mass larger, muscles larger. The female being the nurturer, being that which would be more the caregiver in that sense of softness, bringing in the intuitiveness, the artisan oftentimes is expressed. It is not subservient to the male as each has their equal expression. So that is what would be expressed, each fully aware of their own power, fully able to do the other's task, if necessary. But in the combining of relationship there is that which is the honoring of the differences of one another, and that which brings balance into a relationship or wholeness to relationship. For the relationship is an entity unto itself, just as if it were a being, the male putting the input of the masculinity, and the female the femininity, into the relationship. So there is balance. That is why it is a disservice to blame the relationship for an imbalance when it is the individuals that create it. So what would be addressed in the new time to come in new relationships is a full acceptance of one's power, a full acceptance of one's self, and full responsibility for one's own emotions, and in that there will be a balance for this relationship.

As we move into the spiritual age, people are waking up and putting their foot on a spiritual path, seeking a direct relationship with God. Both males and females share the same challenge in that they are on a path that their spouse or significant other chooses not to go down. What of these relationships when one has chosen the path and their partner has not?

Then is that not an issue for the relationship in communication? And then it is a choice, is it not? For oftentimes one thinks the other must be identical, each in their own way. One would come to their own spiritual alignment. One is not judged, do you see? One cannot judge another's expression or experience for no one can know what another's soul has planned. However, in a partnering or a marriage, as you put it, a coming together, these beings have a specific purpose to learn from one another, and as they grow that may be completed. Then the relationship is complete. In the past, because of the physical structure, there was a finite time of life and the expression of relationship. So there was one marriage oftentimes, and then death. Now with longevity, the physical bodies are stronger, and the beings are taking responsibility so they can be timeless in physicality. They are releasing those issues that create dis-ease. Integration creates healthfulness on all levels, so that then there is a greater time frame of incarnation. One can have many life-learnings or soulful experiences in one body, not needing the relinquishment of the body, continuing on to draw into itself more learning. So one then does not judge another's experience but is fully present within their own and speaking clearly to what is appropriate and inappropriate, to being fully aware of completions, not in judgment, but a going forward into the experiences that their soul draws them. Is there longevity in relationships? There can be. Are there marriages that have longevity? Yes. But it is all on an individual basis. One cannot have a rule, let us say, for the masses. For each one is responsible for their learnings. To take that responsibility allows each being to live fully in the truth of their soul. We are not saying being selfish and self-centered, but centered in self, meaning aware, mindful, communicative, truthful. All of these words are very important in this time to come, and very necessary in relationships, not only marriages, but in all relationships.

How do we really know when a relationship has served its purpose on a soul level, and ifs time to move on?

There is no doubt. When there is completion, it is as if a lightbulb is on or off, or a candle flame burning or not—as clear as this, if one is attentive.

Yet it is difficult because the family is so important to us. Children are often involved. Many people would say that it is better for the children to stay together.

When there is a relation that is complete, it can be destructive to all about them to continue on, for there will be an agitation, attention that is not healthful for any. As to the young ones, as to the children, that is presuming that they are not aware. Know, just because the bodies are small, the soul is not. The soul chooses perfectly an environment to get its highest learning. Trust that. A soul does know and chooses an environment of relationship to learn from, whatever that learning may be. It is more important that the individuals realize that the individuals have relations with one another. A child has a relationship to the mother, regardless of the father. The father has a relationship with the child, regardless of the mother. They are individualized relationships. Yes, they have chosen to interact in a structure, a family, a home, for a period of time. Does not the child grow and leave the home after a certain number of years? Yes. Would the parent wish it not to go forward with its learning? No. The greatest sin, if you would, is that which would block another's growth on a soul level or a spiritual level. So, to encourage soul growth is the most appropriate encouragement.

Yet many people have so much anger and resentment and negative energy attached to the divorce process. How can we transmute this energy?

Is that not from an old patterning of an expectation gone unmet? Oftentimes that expectation has gone unvoiced. Expectations cannot be met unless they are heard. Oftentimes it is an assumption that the expectation will be met by another when it should be met by the self.

Which brings us to the question of forgiveness. Why is it so hard to forgive when an expectation has been unmet?

It is not difficult for forgiveness in release if one takes responsibility for their own feelings and actions. That is what we are speaking to. It seems simplistic, and it is. Much harder to implement, however, because of the old patterns and beliefs of the past.

How can couples nurture their relationship to achieve a greater depth of connection?

Honoring each other. Honoring the individual, the soul. Communicating from mindfulness and soulfulness. Listening and speaking. Being respectful. Loving. Love the self. And that expression of love can be experienced in all relationships. For one cannot love another if one does not love the self. That is the truth that continues on year after year after year, moment after moment after moment. That will not change.

Do you see more or less emphasis on the institution of marriage as we move into the new millennium?

Connectedness, commitment, will continue. Commitment on a soul level and the expression of that soulful commitment will be addressed in marriage. Marriage is a structure for the family as well as a relationship of male and female, or a loving relationship; connectedness. As to more emphasis? There has always been an emphasis on this and it will continue. Emphasis is on the desire of connection, one unto the other. And that is a continuum for that is part of the earthly experience.

We know that God is not a judgmental God, but many people place religious importance on the institution, or the sacrament of marriage. Is that something God cares about?

It is the choosing of the soul, you see. God does not judge it. It is the commitment of the soul. It is that which is the unconditional loving expression of God that is the gift. As to the sacrament of marriage, as to the legalities of marriage, those have been made by man. The soul knows commitment. The soul knows truth. The soul knows love. If one is fully soul-realized then there is the fulfillment of commitment.

There is a lot of judgment today placed on homosexual relationships. Why is there such judgment about homosexuality?

Fear. Most often those that are most fearful of that expression are not secure and centered within themselves. Those who hold great fear and judgment of others have been mirrored unto that insecurity within, meaning that those that are most fearful wish not to have that expressed in their environment because they are fearful of that within their own being, and that they perceive in some way that it is wrong.

Why is that?

Oftentimes it is a belief that has been instilled or learned. There is no right or wrong here. It is the soul expressing what is appropriate for its growth at the time. As we stated earlier, it is no one's responsibility or ability to judge another's soul's experience. For the soul chooses perfectly what is appropriate for its growth. Those who would judge another don't know the soul's purpose. Correct? They are judging another's path by their own fear-based emotion, their own fear-based intellectual thinking, not from a soulful or mindful place, not from a fully integrated place. If one is fully integrated in themselves and taking full responsibility for themselves, they would not want to judge another, they would not be going outside themselves to judge another, thinking it their responsibility.

What is the biblical justification for this judgment?

They have chosen to perceive statements in their own mind thinking, intellectual thinking, and assuming that it is a meaning for this particular endeavor. It could be read in many different ways; it does not speak specifically. The interpretations of the biblical stories and words have been misconstrued. There are truths within this book, but one must discern the core or the truth that resonates, for it is known that it was written many years past the events. It is known to be written by personalities that have their own issues emotionally. It has been also transcribed by individuals, human beings, and their own influences. So one must discern what the truth is.

Is homosexuality a choice that is made before incarnating?

At times.

What are the factors that influence one's sexual preferences?

There are many different factors, there are emotional factors, there are physiological factors, there are spiritual or soulful factors, and they may be all in one being. Or there may be one or the other. It is individualistic. But know, the soul has chosen a particular body for a particular experience, whatever that may be. If it is a body that is physiologically and hormonally and energetically balanced to one or the other, then the soul has chosen that path for a particular reason, whatever that may be. It may be the interactions of the people they come in contact with, not necessarily the experience of the physical sexual orientation.

Does this apply to both males and females?

Yes. So we cannot say specifically it is one way or the other.

So to clarify, it can be genetic, it can be on a soul level, it can be influenced by the psychological, the upbringing, all of these factors would play into that?

Yes. And some would have all of them and some would not.

Clearly then, in most cases it sounds as though it would be a choice made by the soul prior to incarnating with the knowledge that that body would have a sexual preference that would be challenging for them within society?

Possibly. Oftentimes the soul chooses a particular environment not because of that, but because of the interaction of the personalities or souls they will interact with. It is then expressed in a particular way.

Is the perception that society has had of homosexuality changing now with the movement into a higher place of nonjudgment and acceptance?

Know that there are certain segments or sections of society and not others that judge it.

Clearly, but as we move down the road into the spiritual age, the age of Soul Integration, it would seem likely that we would be witnessing less judgment or fear surrounding this as with anything that has been fearful to us.

Correct. So then does that not change to a higher vibrational frequency the experiences of humanity in a greater community? Loving community?

The common unity?

Correct. Not in judgment of one another, but in love with one another. Very important, yes?

Yes it is. When we speak of spiritual partnering, people are waking up to the opportunity for achieving a higher level of spiritual awareness, or higher consciousness, through their sexual relationship with their partner. How can we achieve these higher states?

As one is integrated on a soulful level and fully in touch with their beingness, there is an openness and vulnerability that does come about that allows the being to be more fully present in the physical structure, and in doing such, more connected. For know that sexuality and interaction and intercourse brings about a connectedness to the God self, to the Creator, and is the closest connection to creation there is. So if one is fully soul-realized, fully soul-integrated, one then experiences their creative forces, their sexuality, their intercourse with their partner, their mate, in a much deeper way and they touch God together, out of that full expression of their soul.

I would ask you to speak more to that in terms of how we can integrate sexuality into our spiritual lives and spiritually into our sex lives.

Attention. Attentiveness. Awareness. Communication. Connectedness. All of these words that we speak here are meaningful in the sense of each being fully responsible for their own emotional maturity, coming together in relationship of preference, not neediness or expectation of another defining or making one whole. In doing such, then the expression of the sexuality can be a dance that heightens awareness, just as meditation does or any other spiritual expression. Sexuality, connectedness to one another, done with respectfulness and attentiveness and love, is that full expression of the soul. It would be attentive, meaning that rather than rushing about when one engages in a loving relationship, that is a part of it. There are many forms of sexual meditations that enhance the being. We speak about the tantric practices of the Eastern societies that have been used for hundreds or thousands of years, for connectedness of partners, of honoring of the masculine and feminine, of their honoring each other. We recommend study of these practices for beings to be fully present in relationship one unto the other, in loving ways, utilizing all forms of meditation, that which is the honoring of the physical body. For it is a loving of the physical expression and experience, is it not? That is why the soul has entered a body, to experience it fully. So it is an honoring of the physical body just as eating properly, exercising, attention to cleanliness. All of these things are an honoring of the vehicle or the physical structure in the experience therein of it. The tantric or sexual act is a part of that honoring. It is also a raising of vibrational frequency to have multidimensional experiences and connectedness one unto the other on a cellular level. Also on a heart, spiritual, and emotional level.

Do you have any thoughts about the role of celibacy and sexuality in achieving enlightenment or full soul integration?

It is the individual choice in beings that are on the path of enlightenment, and will utilize all the tools that their soul desires to achieve that. If a soul chooses to embody into a physical structure an abstinence of their sexuality as a part of that experience of learning, then it is. But that is not for all, you see. It is that awareness of the physicality and the expression therein of it, and the honoring of it, that is important. It brings one into balance, energy balance. We are not saying one way is preferential to another, because it is individualistic. What is most important to become enlightened, is that intent, and the commitment to do the works necessary to achieve that fulfillment.

As we go down the path of full soul integration, is it likely that our sex drive will increase or decrease?

It would be very dependent upon the soul's choice, would it not, for their experience at the time? Certainly there have been great masters and enlightened beings that have been fully sexually active. There have also been great masters who have been celibate. So therein is your answer, is it not, historically? Once again, one cannot judge another's experience for one cannot know what another's soul's path is. That is why it is necessary to honor each being, to honor the self or the soul or the wholeness of being. Then one can honor that in another. And that is the gift.

✤ *Reflections on Relationships*

New patterns for healthy relationships
- Dependent upon relating on a basis of new thought
- Evolution of consciousness allows relationships to come more fully into balance on an emotional level.

Soul Mates
- More than one
- Soul family incarnates together.
  - Same soul age (earth experience)
  - Incarnate time and time again
  - Share and support growth
  - Not always romantic
  - Not always easy. Can be your highest teachers
  - Eternal relationships
  - Similar vibrational frequency

Twin Flames
- Masculine and feminine aspects of the same soul
- Full energetic alignment
- Complete empathetic and heart connection

Relationship between destiny and free will
- Cocreation of the life circumstance
- The soul has a plan, agreements, prior to incarnating.

Role of karma in relationships
- Karma is opportunities for growth.
- Chance to rectify particular circumstances or to learn from experiences
- It is not good or bad.
- Creates tools to shift and change perceptions.

- The educational process of the soul is like the educational process of the mind.
- Completing karmic cycles allows you to move from old patternings in relationships to new, more fulfilling expressions.

Releasing the fear of repeating old patternings in relationships
- Recognize the need for full soul integration.
- Communicate within the self to identify fragmented aspects of the soul that influence those patternings.
- The patterning of beliefs of not being good enough were created in a particular circumstance.
- Recognize the core circumstance that created the pattern, then resolve it from within.
- Acknowledge the worth of yourself. Love yourself enough to transform the pattern into a new way of being.
- Similar circumstances will then be reacted to from new expressions of self-love.

Old patternings that no longer work
- Patterns that stem from lack of self-love, lack of self-worth
- Passivity, the relinquishment of your power
- Expecting another to make you whole or fulfilled, to heal your wounds
- Not taking responsibility for your own emotional maturity
- Usurping another's process of free will
- Being dominant, needing control over another
- Blocking your partner's growth
- Blaming another for your life circumstances

New patternings in relationships
- Entering into a union from preference, not need
- Taking full responsibility for your actions, not blaming the relationship if your life is not working for you

- Promoting each other's growth
- Spiritual partnering
- Having a fulfilling relationship with yourself first

Would you rather be happy or right?
- Needing to be right stems from a patterning of self-righteousness and judgment.
- The need to control another is fear-based.
- Fear of not being heard, acknowledged or loved enough
- Happiness means not having to defend your position, being nonattached to the outcome, yet still speaking your truth.

Conflict resolutions: The choice of anger and judgment versus compassion and acceptance
- Anger is a projection of one's own pain.
- Attempt to always communicate from the heart.
- Listen very carefully. Allow for full sharing of feelings before responding.
- Do not blame. Speak your feelings—"I feel," instead of "You make me feel." No one ever makes you feel or do anything that you do not allow.
- Do not attack. This will result in withdrawal or retaliation.
- Examine the intent behind your words.
  - To hurt or to harm? (Fear based)
  - For resolution or clarity? (Love based)
- Recognize the divinity in "the ability for vulnerability."
  - A true sharing from the heart
  - Not reacting out of ego
  - Will elevate you to the height of genuine humility
  - By sharing your deepest fears, you will disarm the anger and recognize an immediate energy shift.
- When one is acknowledged, there is a feeling of acceptance.
- Remember that you always have the choice in the way you act and react.

Spiritual Partnerships
- A relationship with a purpose
- Allows for the learning of the soul and the integration of the self?
- One mirrors unto the other perfectly what is necessary for each other's growth.
- There is a recognition of an eternal connection.

The masculine and feminine roles in the new millennium
- The feminine
  - The internal, intuitive expression of the soul
  - The expression of spirit
  - The nurturer
- The masculine
  - The protector
  - The outer expression of the soul
    - The warrior
    - The provider
- Roles have been dictated by physicality and necessity, not by society.
- Humanity is now integrating masculine and feminine aspects of self. Becoming whole.
- There is no less judgment for men of this recognition and integration of both energies within us.
- The dominant/submissive model no longer works.
- It is wise to perceive the relationship as an entity unto itself with equal parts—masculine and feminine.
- Honor the differences in one another.

Relationships with partners on different spiritual paths
- Strong need for communication
- Expectations must be expressed.
- Must honor each other's path and need for growth
- It is inappropriate to judge another soul's expression or experience.
- Physical longevity creates opportunity for many life-learnings and soulful experiences.
- The completion of a relationship should not be judged.
- Each partner should be aware, mindful, communicative, and truthful.

How do we know when a relationship is completed?
- Ultimately there is no doubt—it is as if a light is on or off.
- You can feel it on the deepest levels of your being, if you are attentive and aware.

Is it better for the children involved to stay together?
- When a relationship is completed, it is destructive for all to continue on.
- Agitation and lack of love will be known and felt by the children.
- The relationship between each parent and the children should not end.
- Each soul knows and chooses an environment to get its highest learning—trust that.
- The patterning of staying in a loveless relationship would be more damaging.

The institution of marriage
- Connectedness and commitment on a soul level
- Excellent structure for the family
- Excellent expression of a loving relationship

- Man-made institution, not judged by God
- The soul knows commitment, truth, and love, with or without a marriage.

Homosexual relationships
- Judgment is fear based.
- Those who hold great fear and judgment of others have mirrored to themselves that insecurity within.
- Judgment is typically a belief that has been instilled or learned.
- There is no right or wrong with regard to sexual preference.
- It is the soul expressing what is appropriate for its highest growth.
- Fully soul-integrated beings would not feel the need to judge another's experience.
- Interpretations of the biblical stories and words have been misconstrued.
- There is less judgment and more acceptance now in the new millennium.

Spirituality and sexuality
- Sexuality and interaction and intercourse bring about a connectedness to the God self—to the Creator. It is the closest connection to creation there is.
- Touching God together out of the full expression of the soul
- Sexual meditations are profoundly nourishing.
- Tantric practices of Eastern societies allow partners to be fully present in a relationship in loving ways.
- Tantric and meditative practices can raise one's vibrational frequency to have multidimensional experiences and connectedness to one another on a cellular level.

Chapter 4

Children and Parenting

*"Transforming the historical family patterns
allows the children to be
fully who they are, not acting out the
patterns of the past."*
—THEO

Many family patternings that have been passed down for generations are no longer working in this time of high transformation. Children and young adults, to follow their own soul's path, are now breaking free of the conditionings and expectations placed upon them by their parents. As many of us know, this is not always easily accepted and can create great turmoil within the family structure. It is, however, necessary for children and parents alike to recognize the need to celebrate each other as both teachers and students. The learning now is not only for the children.

THEO tells us, "Heal the parents and the children will be fine." As parents take full responsibility for their own emotional growth, they will empower their children to be who they really are. As parents authentically live their spiritual beliefs, they allow their children to purposefully develop their own.

As THEO has often stated, the soul chooses perfectly those life experiences that are necessary for its highest learning. This applies, of course, to the parents and family environment that it chooses prior to incarnating. It is difficult for our linear minds to fully understand, but THEO compares this selection process to that of choosing an academic curriculum. The soul then cocreates the life experience ultimately with the conscious mind, for therein lies the learning.

It is wise for us as parents not to be fooled by the young age of our children, for in that small body may reside a very old soul, a great teacher. THEO speaks of older souls as those that have had more earth experience and are typically the teachers and facilitators for spiritual growth. Younger souls are described as those with less earth experience that continue to create karma, or circumstances out of their own insecurities, greed, and narcissism, that are ultimately necessary for their growth. We are told that many older souls are now incarnating to participate in this time of the new millennium, the Spiritual Age.

Most of the rules for effective parenting haven't changed. Children need structure, protection from physical harm, boundaries to understand the negotiable and nonnegotiable rules, and consistency in the enforcement of the consequences of their actions. They also need to be heard, honored, and loved, and to see and feel compassion, kindness, and caring patterned by their parents. It is also inappropriate for parents to project their own immature emotional patternings on their children, as is frequently the case with divorced parents. That which is the highest good of the children must always be the first priority.

We encourage all parents to recognize the family patternings that were most beneficial in their own upbringing, while shedding those that were not, as they create their own parenting style. It is imperative to remember that the children now are very bright, possibly feeling a little confined by their young bodies, and need us, as parents, to acknowledge them as the beings of wisdom that they are.

I've heard you say many times, as relates to children and parenting, that if you heal the parents, the children will be fine. Could you elaborate, please?

In that which would be the adults, the parents of young children coming into fulfillment of their soul, meaning that they are fully soul integrated and realize then that one would find that there would not be the projections of the familiar, or family patterns, that have been brought forward to be visited upon the child. Meaning that the child then could "be," or the soul of that child fully implementing its own decisive path rather than acting out the necessities or the emotional learnings of the parents; that the parents take full responsibility for their own emotional healing, own emotional responses, their own emotions, and then the children would be free to be who they are.

What is the most effective way for parents to provide spiritual guidance for their children?

By living one's own spirituality, or belief, or faith. Children learn by example. By your deeds, they know who you are. They trust who you are. Again, we speak in terms of a child's soul, which can be of any age. Because the body is young, or small, does not mean the soul is. So the soul will seek out its own level of spirituality for that is purposeful in the adventure of the human experience. However, as one would perceive, a soul chooses an environment in which to get its highest learning. So, if one is choosing a particular environment, with a particular parental structure, family structure, religious structure, the soul has chosen that environment to learn from. That which would be best is to live fully one's own belief, to live it, to be integrated in it, to live their truth specifically, and the child then learns from the parent, does it not?

Does the soul choose its parents prior to incarnation?

Yes. The soul, or child, as it were, as you would perceive it, chooses its environment, its parental structure, chooses specific parents, male and female, to interact with. For you would find in a family structure there are times when a child may be more attached or more energetically aligned with one parent or the other. There are those circumstances that a child may be born into *a* family that they are only aligned to the father or the mother, or possibly even a sibling. That is individualistic, do you see? There are circumstances when a child is birthed by a personality, fathered by a personality that they do not engage with as parents. They engage with parents that choose them, that cannot birth. Hereto, it is the child's choice, for there is a knowing. The soul is fully aware.

How is it possible that the learning of the soul is known prior to incarnation?

If one is in an educational system, say a university, there is a catalog of instruction, is there not? For each university, and within that university each educational cell, or that which would be a path, and within that there is a catalog of experiences to be had, to be chosen. It is very similar to that in a broader view. The soul is aware of particular things that it desires out of an incarnation into a human existence. So there are myriad factors that are chosen, such as place of birth, people to engage in family with, life circumstances, other people to engage with in the life path, other opportunities of growth that the soul wishes and desires that one could then manifest, cocreatively, once in the body with others. So there are variables, as it might be seen. But that is how one's mind's eye can have an understanding.

If the soul knows prior to incarnation the opportunities that it's going to experience, this would be another example of the absence of time and space, wouldn't it?

There is no time and space on the soul level. When one is choosing, there is an ultimate knowing of one's process, so to speak—not the outcome fully because that is what the learning is about—but that which would be the path, that which would be the choices to be made about what it is that one desires. And then when one is born, the soul continues to cocreate with the human existence those opportunities for growth.

Is there anything you can add to that?

It is a very broad stroke here but you would find that the conscious mind could not perceive the enormity of opportunity or choice. There are millions of choices, trillions of choices, if one would look at it. But the soul is very aware and can delineate as you would if you are looking upon your computer for opportunities. It would be vast. However, there is a knowing of a particular thing that you want so then you place it in an environment in which it comes to your screen and then there is the information. Think in terms of this: selection.

What else can you add regarding what patterns can be changed within the family structure to create the most constructive environment for child rearing?

Communication. Not blaming. Not harsh, meaning abusive. It is to recognize that the adults take full responsibility for their own emotional maturity and not pass along their particular issues onto the child, to allow the child to flourish in their own energy and their own perceptions, allowing responsibilities to be taken, allowing the growth in that way. A parent is a director, a teacher. A child is a teacher, and a student as well, as the parent is a student. Each learns one from the other. But the gift that is given unto a child is the allowance to be who they are, to make choices and to have opportunity to manifest those choices. A parent is there to guide and to protect from harm, a gift of truth, communication, sharing, knowledge, befriending, being a friend, nonjudgmental.

I think the dance for parents is to know when to allow the child their own learning...

Always.

The dance that I ask you to speak to is that of moving from protecting to allowing. How can parents do both at the same time?

There is protecting from physical harm, and communication is a key, educationally speaking, to a young one; and being aware of age, as well, in the process of growth and the maturation. Allowing one to take responsibility for one's choices, that is how the learning is done. If a parent is fully understanding of their own responsibility within themselves, they model that and have an intuitive guide from their own process, giving strength to the child to be their own person. The parent who has not taken the responsibility from within the self, and lives through the child, oftentimes that child can be either neglected or overprotected and usurp their will to learn. So one, as a parent, should be vigilant in their own learning and their own expression, and their words, to be attentive.

Are children vibrating at a higher frequency, higher than any generation that has ever been on this planet?

Some are, some are not. It is to recognize, however, a child from infancy, from birth, is dependent upon the parent for life, physically, not spiritually. The soul is very strong and it is not young, necessarily, when it is in the small body. However, in a physical existence, in this physicality, the small infant body is dependent upon the parent for life. When it is most sensitized is when it feels threatened that it would not have life, or continue, because of that dependency. So when one asks if children are more sensitized, yes, because of that dependency for life early on. However, in some circumstances, that need or sensitivity becomes distorted and carried on into adulthood. The fears, the sensitivity to abandonment, are great. And that is herein many of the issues in relationships. So that is why parents should be cognizant of that dependency and that hyperawareness and sensitivity—it means survival. Now, if a parent is very sensitive to this, a parent can support this young body, let us say, this young personality and the soul by communication, letting it know it is loved, letting it be in the truth of its being. That gives great support.

Do children become only as conscious as their parents until they grow to the age where they are more aware of their opportunities?

Yes. But there are those young ones that are old souls that come in smaller bodies that can teach younger soul parents. But that is another issue.

Speak more to that, please.

There are different soul ages embodied upon the earth. Personalities that come for particular learnings. Older souls have more experience. They are teachers. They are facilitators of growth of spirit and enlightenment. Younger souls, having not the earthly experience and the learning of emotions, continue to create karma, or circumstances out of their own insecurities, their greeds, their narcissism, for growth. Oftentimes, they come across an older soul as a child, so that older soul can lead them and teach them, even though they are younger, by different experiences. However, the older soul is fully aware of that, that they are the parent, not the child in those circumstances. However, it is to recognize that as beings move forward into this new time, this new millennium, this new expression of fulfillment and self, there's a greater awareness. And as beings take full responsibility for their own personal integration and integrity, then that gives freedom for all about them to be who they are.

Children are going to act out and require discipline when their behavior is inappropriate. How do parents most effectively and appropriately discipline their children?

Young ones need structure to feel safe and secure. Consistency in that structure. Communication. It is taught early on to take responsibility for one's actions and reactions, meaning that when one is a child there needs to be in that structure, in place, as we stated earlier, for every action there is a reaction. There should be rules to live by; that is structure. So there are boundaries so there is a sense of security. Boundaries are very important; "This is appropriate action, this is not. This is negotiable, this is not." These are ways of the world, of teaching a child to interact in day-to-day activity as an adult, it is not only as a child. Many parents do not have boundaries themselves for that has not been a learning. They are learning it as adults, and have difficulty doing such at times. The gift given unto a child is structure, discipline in the sense of taking responsibility for their actions, whatever they may be, the boundaries we spoke about, negotiable and nonnegotiable rules, communication from the truth of the being. For children know truth.

Again we speak of their sensitivity and their intuitiveness, and their telepathic awareness has meant survival. So to speak the truth, they know it. If it is not spoken to them, then they would not trust. Trust is extremely important in relationships, whether it be with a parent or child, siblings, friends, workmates, partners, marriages. That is what is learned. Communication clearly is the key; listening and speaking truth.

What are your thoughts regarding the consequences of a child's inappropriate behavior?

A relinquishing of their freedom for one thing, for a time, encouraging the inner process in recognition of the action and reaction, withdrawal.

On the part of the parent?

Yes, for that to occur, meaning the inner view with the self.

Speak more to that please... the inner view with the self?

Meaning that the going within to view what was the circumstance, what prompted it, what was the action and reaction, why it was done. When there is that time alone to assess for the self, there is a learning process, privileges to be revoked. Those are earned, as it is with adults. Privileges are earned. It is no different. So what the training does is it gives some insight to a young mind, meaning the intellect. The soul knows much of this, but the intellect does not remember it. So it is remembering. The gift that is given in that structure is the ability to interact in relationship with humanity, not only with the parents, but in the world at large.

At what age are children typically mature enough to be taught soul integration?

That begins early on. However, cognizance or the ability to communicate about it fully is not until they are a bit older, in the sense of education and schooling. There are those who would be able to communicate about it earlier, but they are the older souls that are more fully realized.

You speak about older and younger souls. Since all souls are from the same source, the God source, do you speak in terms of human experiences?

Yes. And when we speak in terms of that in the earthly experience, we are speaking of earth experience specifically. Not to ignore, let us say, opportunities that are not in the physical structure, but when we do speak in these terms, we are speaking of the earthly experience predominantly. For that is what is being chosen to learn from at the moment.

Would "soul age" be the evolution of that soul from the standpoint of learning emotions while in the human experience?

Yes, and also that which is the environment in which it lives, meaning the interaction with other human beings. That is a very broad subject for it takes into account that the earth is but one choice of experience and that there are billions of experiences and teachings not embodied. And there are other universes, there are other planets, other opportunities, let us say. The earth is but one.

What advice do you have for single parents who are raising children on their own?

The rules remain the same. The needs of the child remain the same. Safety, structure, an environment of growth, of the esteem of self, the love of self. So it is as important for all beings, all parents, whether singularly or coupled, to express their own individuality, to take responsibility for their own integration and fulfillment of their soul, and to express that fully. It is no different. As to a parent that is parenting singularly, it is not to demean the other parent, for that does not serve the child.

That seems to be a difficult one for a lot of people in divorce situations.

Even in death. So it is not to project the emotional imbalances of the self onto the child, and not to expect the child to fulfill the self. Very simple.

Same rules as in any relationship, isn't it?

Correct. Only that a child, a young one, is dependent upon the adult for their survival. So it is more important that there is a consciousness about one's interaction with the child, attentiveness, awareness, thought.

We are always fascinated by the group sessions we've done with children. It is beautiful and enlightening for us, as adults, to listen to their questions and see their connectedness. What advice do you have for parents to become more childlike in this way?

To open the heart, to live fully present in the moment-to-moment experience as a child does. An adult is too far into the future or too far into the past and not living in the moment. If one is having difficulty being in the moment, it is then to be aware of what one is speaking, or what one is hearing. To breathe, to feel the breath in the body, allows one to be more fully present in the physical structure. What is one tasting if one is eating? Draw the self back to the experience of that moment. For if you think, "I am thinking about this moment," it is already past, and it is not truly living one's life. If one is in the future, it is not living in the moment and it's passing by a precious gift. If one is too far in the past in the memories, and living only in the memories, one is not in the moment of the present. Ultimately, the memory of the past is tainted because they have not been living in it in the first place. It has been happening to them. So to live one's life fully, it is to be moment-to-moment expressed and experienced, and that in itself is a childlike quality. This is not to say not to have plans for the future. Set those plans, those visions, and let them go. Do what comes moment to moment in your expression and manifesting externally, as you have placed intent on the future through the moment-to-moment expression of life. As all have experienced, as a child, five minutes, thirty minutes, one hour, one day, is an eternity at times. And a year is as if a lifetime. That is full presence that a child has of their life experience moment to moment. Be that aware.

How can we be open to the teachings of children who are perceived to be physically or mentally challenged?

There is an awareness of difference within a child such as this, but there is truly no handicap. There is no difference except in the judgment of others. One can learn greatly from those who are different. That diversity teaches. To watch one grow that is different, to experience life from a different place or a different point of view, or a different experience physically, is a gift. Not to label or to judge others, but to know that their gift is the experience. They are there within that experience on a soul level to gain greatly. So bless them, do not judge them. Give them opportunity to learn and to experience. See the blessing in that one's life that has chosen such a grand adventure, and see how many are touched by them and learn great things from them. Great teachers choose those environments, and it can be seen.

✤ *Reflections on Children and Parenting*

Heal the parents and the children will be fine
- Parents taking responsibility for their own emotional growth
- Children being free to be who they really are
- Children not acting out the emotional problems of their parents

Most effective ways for parents to provide spiritual growth for their children
- By living their own spirituality and beliefs
- Teach by example.
- Recognize that just because the body of a child is young, the age of the soul may not be.
- Know that each soul chooses an environment in which to get its highest learning.

Each soul chooses its parents
- Has a "blueprint" from which it chooses for learning
- May be more aligned with one than the other

How is it that the learning of the soul is known prior to incarnation?
- Similar to a catalog of instruction
- Our conscious minds not being able to grasp the enormity of choices available
- To understand, we would have to perceive beyond linear time, for the soul is timeless.
- There is an ultimate knowing of one's process but not the outcome fully, for in that is the learning, a cocreation with the conscious mind.

Patterns necessary for most constructive child-rearing environment
- Communication
- Not blaming or being harsh
- Parents taking responsibility for their own emotions

- Giving children the gift of allowing them to be who they are
- Recognizing the child and parent as both teacher and student
- Giving the gift of truth
- Sharing knowledge
- Practicing being nonjudgmental
- Protecting from physical harm

How do parents both protect and allow their children their highest learning?

- Allowing children to take responsibility for their actions
- Empowering them to recognize their own process and intuitive guidance
- Giving strength to the child to be his or her own person
- A parent not living through the child
- Parents being vigilant in their own learning, their own expression, and words

When the child is an older soul than the parent

- Older souls have more experience. They are the teachers and facilitators for spiritual growth.
- Younger souls have less earth experience and continue to create karma, or circumstances, out of their own insecurities, greeds, and narcissism for their growth.
- Frequently the child is more the teacher, the older soul, than the parent.
- Chronological age has nothing to do with soul age.

Appropriate disciplinary techniques

- Giving children structure to feel safe and secure
- Establishing and honoring consistent boundaries
- Teaching children that for every action there is a reaction; learning consequences for actions
- Parents teaching negotiable and nonnegotiable rules of the home and of the world

- Parents setting boundaries for their own lives
- Communication, listening, and speaking the truth
- Parents recognizing that children know the truth and their trust is dependent on this

Consequences for actions
- Relinquishment of freedom and privileges
- Encouraging the inner process of recognition of the action and reaction
- Withdrawal from the environment

Single and divorced parents
- The rules remain the same.
- Create an environment for the growth of the esteem and self-love of the child.
- Do what serves the child. Do not demean the other parent.
- Do not project the emotional imbalances of the self onto the child.
- Parents cannot expect the child to fulfill the parent.
- Parents must remember that the child is dependent on them for their survival.

How parents can become more childlike
- Opening the heart
- Being fully present in the moment-to-moment experience as a child is

Children perceived as physically or mentally challenged
- Older souls, great teachers, teachers of compassion and nonjudgmental

Chapter 5

Spirituality

*"Humanity is beginning to understand that which would be the
unification of thought and spirit. Illumination."*
—THEO

Your soul is your greatest teacher. Soul is the essence of your
being that possesses all the wisdom and memories of all
experiences in and out of the human form. It is the energy that is a
spark of and directly connected to the energy of God, your Creator. It
is the Kingdom of God, which does not reside anywhere outside of
you, and no one but yourself is going to lead you to it. Meditation is
the way to have this direct personal experience, connecting with your
soul and being in direct communion with God. We like to refer to it as
our daily "home churching." We are confident that it will change your
life for the better. As an Indian Rishi once stated: "Enlightenment is an
accident, meditation makes you more accident-prone."

There are many authentic spiritual teachers on the planet today.
Regular prayer and/or meditation and the belief that the soul is
eternal are taught by them all. Many teach that the soul is energy and
that each one is uniquely perfect and divine with its own vibrational
frequency, its own unique blueprint, so to speak. They teach that the
choices we make in our lives and the spiritual teachings that we
practice affect this frequency in either a positive or a negative way and

that the higher the frequency, the more we manifest experiences that include connecting with the higher frequency spiritual dimensions, bringing heaven to earth. Ultimately, the responsibility for getting there is yours, but as you are ready, and in the asking, these teachers will show up in many different forms and experiences.

As we have said, the energetics present in this third millennium make possible opportunities for us to access the highest frequency of the soul, the Christ consciousness. Further, these energetics create an environment within which all can have a direct, personal experience with God. But, as we have also said, it's all about full soul integration. As you have a direct path to God through your soul, the idea of the return of a savior or messiah is obsolete. You become our own "savior" in your decision to pursue full soul integration.

THEO speaks of love as pure energy that gives no charge to judgment, confusion, or separation. They speak of it as being the full resonance within the soul. They define it as the spiritual frequency that creates miracles. The shift from fear to love is now under way.

More and more people are awakening to a desire for spiritual purpose in their lives. Organized religion thrives on providing an environment where people can gather in community. We believe, however, that the churches and spiritual organizations that will experience the most growth will be those that honor—and even teach—the direct personal experience with God. The better churches will not teach fear of the nonphysical dimensions; they will recognize multidimensional experiences and methods of enlightenment as processes of soul integration. Patterns of control that promote fear and judgment in our religious institutions will be increasingly intolerable.

THEO tells us that this spiritual age is a time of doing as Jesus did. The miraculous healings and other Holy and magical experiences now being reported all over the planet are a testament to this possibility. We all now have the choice to live as he did, to be impeccably kind and loving, to be healers and teachers, to love ourselves enough to love our neighbors.

Who or what is God?

The creator of your universe, that which is the creation of the human expression, the animals, the flowers, the earth itself. It is that which is the spark of creative force in all things; vibrational frequency; alignment to all things. It is connectedness. It is the expression of humanity; creativity, on all levels.

How do we develop a personal relationship with God?

It is that which is a meditative state on a regular basis allows one to be in alignment to the creative force inside, that then allows a personal experience with that energy, and awareness of it. Belief, faith, all of these words are useful in the mind, but it is experiential as well, as a sense of feeling throughout the entirety of the body. It is that ecstatic feeling of attunement or at-one-ment with all things. It is the revelation of a higher expression of self, meaning that when one is fully in the heart, fully in the soul there is a connectedness to God and that experience is a vibrational frequency in the cellular structure of the body as well. It is a sensory perception.

Is this the illumination of which you speak?

Illumination is radiance as well as a knowing, as well as an awareness. It is many faceted. It is a part of that, yes, but not in totality.

What is the definition of the unification of thought and spirit?

That would be illumination, would it not?

Is there anything you can add to that?

It is experiential. We have not words that can define, for it is that full experience of the being—that is certain. There is an awareness when it is experienced, you see? There are not words to define fully other than ecstasy. Even at that, that is limiting, is it not?

There is so much confusion surrounding who or what God is. Why doesn't God just settle the issue once and for all and make His presence known beyond a doubt?

His presence is known. It is an awareness that is necessary for the consciousness of humanity to receive. It is the responsibility of humanity to come to the full awareness of God, not God explaining it. It is an experiential process, do you see, coming into at-one-ment. Atonement, many call it, but it is completeness, it is full awareness. That is the responsibility of the soul and the individual.

Can you define the Spiritual Age?

Do you not find it very interesting that oftentimes the ages of the past have been defined historically by others who did not live in them and given them a name? Now it is prior to the experience that a name is given to a particular time frame in human history. Very interesting, is it not? That which would be the Spiritual Age, or defined as New Age by some, for it is not so new, it is that which is a recognition and a remembering of the full soul. And in that a requirement, as it were, to humanity being aware of the spiritual aspects of being, meaning that there is experience of the soul so then one becomes aware of their spiritual connectedness that they are not that which is a human being but a spiritual being through experiential process; that this is but one experience in the human body that can be chosen over and over again, but it is but one opportunity of growth and it is not the be-all and end-all of experiences. So this is a time when there will be that full-conscious realization and the desire of humanity because of experience, in the desire of connectedness, will go forward to that greater alignment.

People speak of the present time as a time of spirit merging with the physical. Are we becoming spirit? Is this now a time when there is no separation between spirit and physical matter?

That is a time of recognition, if you would, or remembrance that there is that which is the spiritual being inhabiting a physical structure. So it is that full acknowledgment that the beings are spirit. The body is physical and aligned to the earthly experience. But the spirit is not limited to it. Spirit is used in many different vernaculars. We prefer to speak in terms of soul. The soul is the spirit of which you speak about.

Is the soul merging into or becoming one with the physical body or is it a separate vibration f

The soul is apart of the physical body. A soul chooses an incarnation. But what comes about in this time is a realization on a conscious level of the soul being in the physical body, but not limited to it, beings being fully aware that there has been a choice of a physical existence, and that the soul enters into a physical body, vibrationally speaking. But it can be in and out of that physical structure. The soul has that capability, not limited only to one physicality or to one dimension, but can have experiences, multidimensionally speaking, and be aware of them. So this time or this age, as you speak about it, will be that remembering or awareness in a conscious way that this can be, through a remembering of experience, an inner communication.

You have said many times that God resides within each and every one of us. That spark of God. Could you please explain?

You can speak of it as the Holy Spirit; the breath of life; the creativity in each one; the connectedness that can be experienced in the sense of energy, as many experience in telepathy or connectedness with each other, and with the earth, and with all living things.

But we are also speaking of the soul as the spark of God. They are the same, correct?

Yes.

How is organized religion going to play into the Spiritual Age, and is it heading in a direction of teaching their followers to make their own direct connection with God?

Know that religions will be changing dramatically as well as political structures. All the patterns of the past that no longer serve will change. Religion in and of itself will change as well, to encourage personal relationship. And you will watch as beings flock unto these teachers, because they desire confirmation of what they are experiencing. The old structures were speaking of this connection, for it was taught before, but out of the necessity of controlling the masses. Then as beings had personal experience they were told they could not. So there was this duality, was there not? So what comes about in this time is that beings will have religious affiliations, for they will come together in like thought and gatherings of like thought and teaching. This is the human way, to share. However, it will be expanded experientially.

Why is there fear and judgment associated with some forms of organized religion?

Because the religions are humans, are they not? The structures of the religions have been human made, so, they are as fallible as the humans in charge. For the humans project their own insecurities, their own fears, their own beliefs into the organization. It is not only in the church or in the religion. It is throughout their lives. As beings integrate and come more fully into the wholeness of themselves, they relinquish the need of judgments of others and come about compassionately, for the human experience, an understanding that the soul manifests perfectly what is appropriate for its growth and it is improper to judge another's experience. For only the soul judges, and must take responsibility for its choices.

Please explain the relationship between Jesus the man, and the Christ energy or the Christ consciousness.

Jesus, a human being, born of the flesh, yes as you are, as all humans are born of the flesh. The Christ energy is an energy frequency of a higher vibration that allows the full soul to integrate, to be fully realized, and to be expressed upon the planet. This energy, the Christ energy, fully in place two thousand years past, to be implemented through this teacher, to give the words out to lead humanity into this higher conscious state. However, the beings embodied at the time were not ready to fully realize their potential. Now, in this time, there is that Christ energy fully in place about the earth and beings, humanity, will realize that potential. It is time. They have been preparing for many years, have they not?

We have. But why the misunderstanding about the man Jesus and the Christ consciousness?

Beings wish to place responsibility externally, outside themselves, rather than to bring it within. So then in the belief of human beings, some human beings that were great orators, and great leaders, and charismatic leaders, placed their beliefs on others of what they believed were the truths of God, and of the Christ energy or the man Jesus, who was a teacher. There is great emphasis put upon the man Jesus continually, but have there not been great teachers and masters upon this planet as well? He was one. Do you understand? All energetically aligned teachers, all spiritually aligned teachers and leaders for this world in the sense of alignment to God and angelic beings coming forth to share enlightenment with humanity, high vibrational frequency. Jesus, the man, had these capabilities and abilities refined and defined, and had the ability to integrate fully his soul and to be this teacher. Many did not want to try their own experiences, for they were fearful. So they placed all of the responsibility of God's message, God's words, Godly teachings onto him, rather than listening clearly unto the words that empowered humanity to embrace the God self. That was his teaching. His acts were that to confirm that all human beings, all humankind, had the ability to manifest, to create, to be of great strength and awareness, that they were spiritual beings.

Thus the statement "All that I do, you can do and more." Are we at a time of realizing the magnificence of that statement in our lives now?

Yes, and it has been true throughout history. There have been those who have the ability of manifestation and the ability to utilize their soul and their God energy, should we say? However, it is a time now fully upon this planet for the masses to be in realization of that empowerment. The beings, the human beings, humankind, will be asking for it, because they are glimpsing, they are experiencing, they are having profound experiences that lead them to the questioning and the desire to know intellectually, consciously.

How can we begin to manifest these abilities, these powers in our lives?

First off is the desire, the intent and the awareness to it. The utilization of manifestation is that which is the full awareness of one's personal power, and how one achieves that is through self-acceptance, self-love, meditation. These are all words that have been told over and over and over again to humanity. But it is important that beings implement, integrate themselves, to relinquish the beliefs that they are not good enough or lovable enough for this to occur. And as this is done, their experience expands and they too can do these deeds unencumbered from the past beliefs.

Are there some specific training or skills that we need to develop, or teachers who can teach us how to do this?

There are. Yes. But most importantly it is going within and integrating on a soul level; becoming aware of the fragmented parts of the self and bringing them home; relinquishing those beliefs of not being good enough through process of integration; and in that, a self-love evolves that allows one to be centered in the self, whole within self.

The Christ energy that Jesus embodied, was there a particular time in his life when it entered and then left his body?

Twelve. And the specific alignment to the energy of integration continued on with him. But as to the energy that you speak of, as the teacher upon the planet, ended at the Crucifixion.

When Jesus spoke of the Kingdom, what was he speaking of?

The Kingdom of God? It is that which would be the beings realizing the Kingdom is the soul.

So there isn't any place that we need to go?

There is a place you need to go: fully into the wholeness of being, which then is the realization of God, which then is the Kingdom of God. It is an energetic frequency, it is a dimensional frequency, it is alignment, it is many things that we could speak about and give you words such as these for an understanding, but then as words are spoken then it brings up more questions about other words, does it not? It is an experiential at-one-ment or attunement to the wholeness of self.

How do we remain aware of and embrace this divine presence in every moment of our lives?

Be conscious of it. Intend it. Attend to it. Become it. Live it.

Are there any writings today, or will we be finding or uncovering any writings that were directly from Jesus?

Jesus did not know how to write. He was an orator, a speaker, he did not write. Others wrote many years past him. His tools were that of carpentry, not writing. His ability to speak to others, his charisma, his energetics, his healing capabilities were energetics that were about him and through him. It was not written.

Can you share with us some of the important aspects of his childhood and where he received his training prior to his public ministry f

It was fully realized by those of awareness who this being was. In the sense of a soul level, an older soul, one that had great wisdom, one that had an energetic frequency as a healer and a teacher. It was seen by what would be called the elders but, more importantly, you could speak of them as the trainers of this personality, that knew the skills from the human perspective, that he would need to share with the world. They groomed him.

Who are they?

The Essenes.

What can you tell us about the Essenes?

The Essenes were high-vibrational-frequency souls that were embodied as teachers, guides, and mentors for humanity in that time. They came upon the planet for the high energetic shift that was happening for humanity in that time. Fully aware, angelic beings.

Where else did Jesus get His training?

There were many prophets about in that time that knew of his coming, and they foretold it. There was also the Sanhedrin, which was the religious teachings. He needed to know the religion of the area in which he would teach so that he could speak the words that were comfortable for these beings, acceptable.

Where did he learn to embody or embrace his miraculous healing powers?

He knew that he had them. He had experimented with animals. He could touch them and they would be healed. That was seen early on, his capabilities with his energetics. But it was not only his hands-on works, but the energy that permeated his body. Many think of the auric field, radiant. He radiated this energy and this charisma and when one was in his presence there was a full awareness of his ability, and then it was the asking of those about him to touch them. When in the presence of a master, one knows it.

Did Jesus, in his earlier years, spend time in India and Egypt learning specific techniques to be able to manifest these miracles?

Yes. He had the capability of doing it. He learned the process from those that could do it, as many learn from the masters of today. But more important is that Jesus had the capability and learned how to trust the self through confirmation after confirmation of his ability. That is what the teachers did for him, allowed him to utilize his skills to gain confidence, and protected him.

He could only heal those that believed that he could heal, is that correct?

Correct. And that is true today. In the environment of your world, those that have belief in healing and the capabilities of others to facilitate energy shifting, there can be miraculous healings. But it is known as those that are healers are only facilitators, conduits to the energy frequencies that then can balance the physical body of one that is out of balance. Those that have not the belief do not empower themselves to heal.

Is Jesus going to come back at this time?

The energy is about the earth now and is fully in place in all humanity.

That being the Christ energy?

Yes.

How about Jesus?

The man?

The soul of Jesus.

This man does not need to incarnate again. The energy is fully in place about the earth presently. Humankind have that spark within them and the ability to become it fully.

Would the soul of Jesus then be present from a guidance standpoint?

Yes. As are many of the masters, the teachers, the angelic hierarchy.

Are the twelve apostles returning for this time of magnificent shift?

Yes.

Will they in some way be able to identify each other?

Yes.

And come together?

Yes.

When do you see that happening?

It is happening. Now.

What is Jesus' message for mankind right now?

It has never changed. To love the self fully and to love the neighbor as the self. It is extremely important and it is very simplistic, for if one fully loves the self and is in full soul realization, there will be no judgments, and there will be peace amongst men, and a love of the neighbor, meaning the entirety of the world, and a connectedness of humanity; a common unity, a community of human kind. Family. Fully realized.

Did Jesus advise against drinking alcohol or eating meat?

Yes, to particular personalities, to particular times. Know those words oftentimes were given in particular circumstances to particular groups of personalities of that time. It would be as if a teacher stood before a group that had a particular need or imbalance, it would be discussed that this be relinquished for health sake. So one must discern the messages therein given unto the time, the place, and the beings spoken to. There are truths in the writings, but it is to remember that which rings as truth, that which resonates as truth, is the kernel, is that which should grow within the heart and let the rest drop away.

Is there a lot of truth in Revelations?

There is truth in Revelations, for this is the time of revealing, is it not? It is the time that is spoken about, but not in the sense of devastation. Many preferred to think in terms of the demolition of the earth and the peoples therein of it. Not so. What comes about is the revealing of the whole soul that allows for the change of patternings within the human experience that allows for a greater fulfillment upon the earth. It is the desolation of old patternings. So beings should pay attention to the inner process. For they are looking outside of themselves for this, and it comes from within.

What of Genesis, and the truth contained therein?

It was a good story, was it not? Know that the Bible and these stories were for the mind of man to grasp, for the mind understands through pictures and through experiences; so in story form as descriptive. Then there is an understanding in the consciousness, a relationship to the experience of the story to the human being. For then the human says, "Yes, I understand, because I have experienced a similar experience," or, "I have witnessed a similar experience."

And what of the story of Adam and Eve?

Here too is a story that allows for the human expression, the human body evolved to hold spirit, or soul. It is not literal. It was a story of awakening, was it not? And the duality, yes?

Can you give us an overview of the process that took place in the creation of the Bible?

There are many versions of the Bible. King James is used by a particular sect, or group of religious beings. There are other interpretations that are used by others. So there are some differentiations between them. Know that the Bible in and of itself, these pages, were written and begun to be written at almost one hundred years past the events. So if one would realize that one writes from a perception that was stories given down, time over time, to others and then written out. The memories are of some who did writing as well, for some writers were experiential themselves. But as in any conversation, as in any experience, there is the perception of the writer and their process. So that is why we say the truths lie within the pages. But one must discern from their own being the physical feelings that they have, the knowing they have within their heart, what is the truth that resonates. Is it a literal sense? No, it is not. Can it be taken literally two thousand years after the fact? No, it cannot. For those words and those experiences were given to humanity in a time that was not as highly evolved as now. So it is a disservice to humanity to remain stuck in that dimension, rather than allowing the evolution of consciousness, the ability to discern what is appropriate. The core truth is important. It is very simple. That simplicity has not changed. It is the conscious mind of humanity, or the intellectual mind, that wishes to create something more complex. Seek out the kernel of simplicity, the kernel of truth in all these writings, and there is a consistency, and adhere to that.

Did Jesus, in fact, perform most of the miracles described in the Bible?

He performed many miracles, or what would be deemed miracles, yes. But know as with any society, as with any experience, the story one from another from another does become embellished at times. Or if it is not believed fully, it would be deleted or ignored.

It has been said that Jesus taught reincarnation. Yet it has been written that some references have been stricken from the Bible. Could you please speak to that?

Not all references have been stricken from that Bible, but there has been the deletion of some of this information, that is correct.

And did Jesus, in fact, teach reincarnation?

Spoke to it, yes, that it was life unending, that there was a continuum, and that there was that which would be the choice of the embodiment time and again to assist the learning process of the soul.

Is it true that the soul of Jesus had been incarnated prior to entering Jesus' body?

There have been other incarnations of that energy Jesus. There had been prior to that, in prophetic ways, this being, upon the planet. But it is not an embodiment of this world at this time.

Why are there so many wars fought over religion and God?

It is the interpretations of the Word of God, and the individuals that then wish to say -that their belief is stronger than another's. There is that which is the judgment of one another, one human to another, as to the beliefs that they have, and that their beliefs are wrong and the others are right or whatever would be, in that sense of control and that self-righteousness of the individual. So then there had been factors within those judgments of others that, in turn, believe that the annihilation of another, because their beliefs were not the same, was an important factor to control the planet. Coming into this time, there will be a recognition of that, and there would be a common unity amongst humankind that allows for greater peacefulness of your world, and an understanding one unto the other.

In the book **The Fifth Dimension: Channels to a New Reality** *you say that we have been moving into and are now present in fifth-dimensional energy. Could you explain to us the spiritual realms or dimensions that exist around the earth and how they affect us?*

There are twelve dimensions that are about this earth plane; the third being that which is the physical structure, as you know; the fourth being an awakening to spirit, the fifth being a full implementation of the interaction on the total soul level. And, as this is achieved, there is the sixth, which will be expressed and experienced in the physical structure, which is more shifts of consciousness and a higher vibrational frequency that allows beings to be fully expressing their full spirit upon the earth, and all the modalities of healing, and all the modalities of awareness that are inherent in the experience of a full Soul Integration. The other dimensions are etheric and will be expressed out of the body.

Meaning that we can access those realms while still in the physical body?

There will be some awareness of them, but there would not be the full cogitation of them in the body, for there would not be the expression for it.

When we are out of our body in the astral plane, what dimension are we experiencing?

In the astral, that would be the seventh.

Are there any pictures or words that can be given for an understanding of any realms between the seventh and the twelfth dimensions?

No.

People speak today of the concept of ascension. Can you speak to what ascension is?

Ascension is that which would be the ability to be fully soul integrated and living in that place of fulfillment. Many believe that it is a way of being out of the body. To some it is, but it is that which is important for all beings to be aware if they have chosen a physical structure for their highest learning at this point, it would be appropriate for them to remain in the body. There are many words given, for many take the word or the verbiage of ascension out of the Bible, out of the Christ experience, and express it in those terms.

But that is not really the time that we are in, is it? It is the time of wholeness within the physical body.

Correct.

And do we have the opportunity to leave the body if we choose to forsake of exploration?

Yes.

With our consciousness intact?

Correct.

This is a good time for exploration, isn't it?

Yes. The time is present now. And there are many that go out of the body in an exploratory way and express that which is spirit and interaction with guides and masters. This does occur.

And how can we manifest that in our lives?

The meditational process on a daily basis allows one to be altering of those states or vibrational frequencies so that there can be this experience. It is an integration on a soul level that allows one to be more fulfilled and able to participate.

Is it about placing the intent?

Yes.

And are there any techniques that you can share with us that would facilitate that process in a conscious way?

Place the intent and then to do the meditation without expectation, allowing it to evolve to that which is a time frame, that the body would be at the frequency to allow it.

There's a lot of conversation today about the divine feminine, or the goddess energy. Could you speak to that, please?

It is a recognition of the masculine and the feminine and that which is a blending and acceptance of that which is the feminine and the masculine. The masculine has been given much import, but now there is much notice that there was an imbalance, and there is the necessity of the feminine to be addressed. So there has been much attention given it now. But that is because it has been out of balance. For there is the masculine and feminine energies, the yin and yang, the positive/negative, however one wishes to perceive it. And there is that necessity within each individual to come into balance with those aspects.

Is the feminine a little stronger right now? Is it catching up, so to speak?

Yes. It is being acknowledged.

Would that then be the side of us that would be the more spiritual, the more sensitive, the more emotionally aware?

Yes.

That is permeating us more energetically now? Being activated?

Yes, for men and women. The balance of the feminine is important, for it is the intuitive, the spirit. And that is what is at the forefront at this point.

Many people speak of having experiences with the feminine or with the goddess. To what do they speak?

The recognition of the feminine. The attributes of the feminine or the goddess is that which is intuitive, is healing, it is of high-vibrational frequency that is creative. So there is that creative energy, an energy of birth upon the planet.

Could you explain to us what other universal or spiritual laws affect the earth experience?

There are no absolutes. To understand that there is always expansion and change for humanity; that there can be no absolutes because there is the creation or creativity within the individual, within humanity, that allows for the cocreation of experience in the outer world. So there is a constant change. If one perceives an absolute, that absolute would be change, movement, growth.

What of absolute truths?

There are truths that are consistent. But it is within the interpretation of the individual that they gain insight and acceptance of their truth.

As we move into a higher state of consciousness, will the positive and negative polarities shift accordingly?

There is a continuum of balance energetically, for the polarities are important for balance. However, there is a better understanding that is not to be thought of as good or bad. It is using all the energy that is important for the balance, you see. To come into fulfillment and balance is what is necessary. It does not mean that the negative becomes positive, no. Think in terms of only energy. Not good or bad. When one thinks in terms of negativity, it is thought of as bad. But if personalities would only think in terms of energetics, and that the polarities, when in balance, is good, and that is what is achieved. Working with the positive energy, as well as the negative energy, and knowing how to do that, is the key. And that is what will be learned.

So what is the key to learning that?

Finding within the self an acceptance of the positive and negative inside. The recognition of the polarities of the body bring about healthfulness. It is the acceptance of the masculine and feminine attributes of personality. Not giving credence one over the other, one greater than the other. Equalization.

How do the laws of cause and effect, or karma, relate to our spiritual growth?

Karma is that which is opportunities of growth. So, a karma could be a challenge. A challenge can be that which is an opportunity of growth and experience, of fulfillment when achieved, when faced, when experienced, when brought into balance within the individual.

Could you please explain to us the power of prayer and how to be most effective with our praying?

Prayer is the focus of thought, is it not? Thought is the creative process. Prayer can also be that of gratitude; gratitude is extremely important. It is a recognition of acceptance of that which is desired and manifested. It is a very powerful experience, prayer, whether that be of the asking or of the gratitude. Each is equally important.

Why does it appear that some of our prayers are answered and others are not?

They are all answered.

But they are not always the answers we want.

Correct, because the conscious mind cannot know always what is of the highest good for the being in the moment. For remember, the intellect wishes to maintain control, and the intellect is only a function.

What is the greatest spiritual deed that we can do for humanity?

Love the self. Integrate the soul. Do the inner work of the being to come into fulfillment and balance. And once one has achieved that at-one-ment, or atonement, or attunement, however one wishes to speak of it, when one is one with self, one would be with God, and then there is no judgment, there is unconditional love there that which is a radiance of love. That is the greatest gift that is given unto the world, is it not? So to place intent on an individualistic basis for that to be achieved, brings about the balance, the love, the fulfillment that humanity seeks.

Why does the soul forget prior to incarnation?

It has been in the past that the soul, or the being, or the human experience, was such that the consciousness of humankind could not carry the responsibility within its consciousness of all that had been experienced previously because of the self-judgments and the self-ridicule that has been. When one comes to a place of detachment of that, one can be aware of all experiences that one has had, as opportunities of growth and expansion on a soul level, and the learning of the emotions that have been attached to those circumstances. Then one can accept fully the self. But know that humanity had not been in an evolutionary place to be able to accept all of that previously, and so there needed to be, as one might perceive, veils, or the loss of memories, for one could not carry all that knowledge. Now humanity is evolving in a consciousness way that allows for the ability to detach from the past. And know that it had its purpose and necessity for the soul in an experiential way, and can carry that information forward more directly, not assuming the roles of the past.

How do we create a balance between our work and our spirituality? How do we get more meaning and more depth from our work?

They are not exclusive one unto the other. Know that, as one works in the world, and that means substance and livelihood and survival, that does not stop the spiritual growth. For every activity in one's life is a part of that experience. So in that recognition that in each experience along one's life path, if one is at work or at play or at home or at childbearing, or child rearing—whatever they may be doing in the moment— is a part of one's spirituality, one's growth, one's soul purpose. The soul does not divide into hours of the day, from job to job, to separate from one experience and be present in another. It is all the same.

It's about walking our talk in every aspect of our lives?

Correct.

What is the anti-Christ?

It is the opposite of the Christ, meaning it is the opposite of at-one-ment. It is, as many perceive, the positive and the negative, is it not? The duality. And is there not duality on the earth and within each individual? So there is the Christ and the anti-Christ in each person.

It gives us the opportunity to choose, doesn't it?

It does.

We can choose to be Christ-like, or we can choose to be anti Christ-like.

Correct.

One leads to integration, the other to fragmentation.

Separation. Yes.

Why would anybody choose that?

Lack of self-love.

As we integrate and move into a higher place of consciousness, what is the impact in our daily lives?

Peace. Peace in the body, peace in the life experience; peacefulness and happiness as one would perceive it.

What can you share with us about the practice of forgiveness?

If one is fully integrated, and one has acceptance of self, then there is the ability to forgive others, for there would be nonjudgment. When one perceives that there is the necessity of forgiveness, it is that which is a perception that there has been an expectation that has gone unmet. And one must realize that they are responsible for themselves, not others responsible for them.

What is the role of the technological modalities that are available to us now in achieving spiritual illumination, or whole brain access? How beneficial can these be for us?

They can be beneficial in the balancing and the experience of multidimensional expressions, particularly those tonal qualities or those machines that assist in sound quality vibrations that allow one to arc up their energy and to balance the left/right brain of the body, meaning that then one is more open and receptive to expression and experience. So they do assist some. They do assist all when they are seeking if they so choose the opportunity. Sound is a very strong usage of vibration that allows beings to come into balance. Color is another, vision. Many of the senses—hearing, seeing, tasting—all of these things, all of these senses are a part of coming into balance, and stimulus to them does bring about a higher frequency.

So we have the ability to manipulate our energy, our vibrational frequency?

Yes.

Does it then condition our brain to the knowing of the availability of these higher frequencies which can then be accessed?

Yes. That is correct. What it does is allow the being to then entrain the self to do this naturally. It is a natural thing for the physical body and the spiritual body to do. But the intellect and the consciousness at times needs training to relinquish control.

Please define the Holy Trinity.

Masculine/feminine/child, yes, it is the Trinity of this. The Triad.

Does it all reside within us?

Yes, and it is in the outward structures, for are there not a Mother, a Father, and a Child that influence the patterning of the human life?

Please share your final thoughts on the merging of spirituality and religion in the new millennium?

It is that which comes about, a common unity within humans to bring about a belief of the one God throughout the cultures, throughout the religions of the world. There has been the one God and the belief in that, and it would return again for the wholeness of the world and the human expression. In addressing that comes about nonjudgment one unto the other, and acceptance of the beliefs, and the learnings of all humanity, one not greater than the other, each in the same belief and manifesting the God-source and the soul within the body, now, blessing the earth with this balance and peace.

✤ *Reflections on Spirituality*

Who or what is God?
- The Creator of the universe and human expression; the animals, the flowers, the earth
- The spark of creative force in all things
- Vibrational frequency, alignment to all things
- Connectedness and creativity on all levels

How to develop a deep, personal relationship with God
- Regular meditation
  - allows you to be in alignment to the creative force inside
  - allows for a personal experience and awareness of the energy of God
  - is experiential
  - results in the ecstatic feeling throughout the entire body
  - gives the feeling of attunement or at-one-ment with all things
  - helps achieve a revelation of a higher expression of the self
  - causes a vibrational frequency in the cellular structure of the body
  - enhances sensory perception
- Illumination is
  - a radiance and a knowing, an awareness
  - full-heartedness
  - soul integration—to define it as ecstasy is limiting.
  - unification of thought and spirit

Defining the Spiritual Age and the new millennium
- A time of recognition and remembrance of the full soul
- Awareness that we are more than our physical bodies
- A knowing that the physical body is aligned to the earth but your soul is not limited to it

- An age of experiencing consciousness, multidimensionally, beyond the physical body
- Recognition of your soul as the Holy Spirit, the breath of life, the spark of God
- A time of telepathy and connectedness with each other and all living things

Organized religion in the Spiritual Age
- Will change dramatically as will political structures
- All patterns of the past that no longer serve will change.
- Will encourage personal experience with God
- No longer will there be the necessity to control the masses.
- Relinquishment of the need for judgment of another's experience
- Will promote the understanding that the soul manifests perfectly what it needs for its highest learning

Jesus and the Christ consciousness energy
- Jesus was born of the flesh as are all human beings.
- The Christ energy is a high vibrational energy frequency that allows the full soul to integrate. It is present now in this time of miracles.
- Human beings two thousand years ago were not evolved enough to fully realize their potential.
- Humanity has been preparing for this Christ frequency and is now ready to realize it.
- Jesus embodied the Christ energy and was fully soul integrated, fully soul realized, capable of performing miracles.
- His teachings and actions were meant to empower the people that they, too, could manifest and create as he did.

How we can develop Christ-like abilities
- Desire and intent

- Self-acceptance, self-love, and full awareness of one's personal power
- Daily meditation
- Full soul integration
- Recognition of the soul as the true Kingdom of God

How to embrace this divine presence in every moment of your life
- Be conscious of it.
- Intend it.
- Attend to it.
- Live it.

The childhood years of Jesus
- Trained as a healer and teacher by the Essenes
  - The Essenes were high vibrational frequency souls embodied as teachers, guides, and mentors for humanity
  - Studied with the Sanhedrin so that he would know the religion of the area
  - Taught by the elders and prophets
  - Developed his healing powers by experimenting with animals
  - Studied with East Indian masters *Is Jesus coming back at this time?*
  - There is no need for the soul of Jesus to reincarnate again.
  - The Christ energy is about the earth now and is fully in place. All of humanity has the spark within them.
  - Jesus is present with other spiritual masters, teachers, and the angelic hierarchy to provide guidance.

Jesus' message for mankind today
- It has never changed.
- Love the self fully and love your neighbor as yourself.
- Full soul realization leads to nonjudgment and peace for all.

- A common unity, a community of humankind. Family. Fully realized.

The truth of the Book of Revelation

- The revealing is not one of devastation or demolition of the earth.
- What comes about is the revealing of the whole soul that allows for the change of patternings, bringing about fulfillment for humanity.
- It comes from within, not outside of ourselves.

The story of Genesis

- New and Old Testaments were written and rewritten by human beings with human patternings.
- There are nuggets of truth contained therein.

Spiritual dimensions about the earth

- There are twelve dimensions about the earth plane.
- The third dimension is the physical structure.
- The fourth dimension is the awakening to spirit.
- The fifth dimension is a full implementation of the interaction on the total soul level.
- The sixth dimension eventually will be recognized and expressed as an even higher vibrational frequency on earth.
- The other dimensions are etheric and are expressed out of the body.
- When consciousness temporarily is out of the body experiencing the astral plane, it is in the seventh dimension.

Out-of-body exploration

- You can journey beyond the physical body in an exploratory way for the expression of spirit and interaction with guides and masters.

- There is much learning in these experiences.
- Meditation allows you to raise your vibrational frequency to achieve these states.
- Place the intent without expectation.
- Allow the process to manifest in its perfect time.

The divine feminine or goddess energy

- It is a recognition of the blending and acceptance of the masculine and the feminine energies.
- There has been an imbalance and the feminine is now being acknowledged.
- This aspect of being is the more spiritual, intuitive, and emotionally aware.
- High vibrational frequency is the healer and the creative.
- It is the birthing of new thought.

Universal spiritual laws that affect the earth

- There are no absolutes, for there is always expansion and change for humanity.
- There is always creation or creativity in each individual.
- If you could perceive absolutes, they would be change, movement, and growth.

Will the polarities shift with humanity moving into higher consciousness?

- There is a continuum of balance, which is necessary for the polarities.
- Do not think of it as good or bad.
- The negative will not become a positive for energy is only energy.
- Acceptance of masculine and feminine aspects of self brings about equalization and healthfulness.

Karma/cause-and-effect in relationship to spiritual growth
- Karma is opportunities for growth.
- There is fulfillment when the experience of growth is achieved due to embracing the learnings and challenges.

The power of prayer
- Prayer is the focus of thought.
- Thought is the creative process.
- Gratitude is extremely important.
- Prayers are always answered but not always in a way the conscious mind expects.

Why your soul forgets prior experiences upon incarnating
- Until now human consciousness was not able to carry the responsibility.
- There is sometimes too much self-judgment and self-ridicule.
- You now are able to let go of the past and accept the responsibility inherent in the wisdom of your soul.

Spirituality and work
- All activities including work are soul experienced and guided.
- Live your spiritual beliefs in every activity.

The anti-Christ
- The choice you make in every moment of your life
- The opposite of Christ-like, or at-one-ment
- Represents the duality of the earth experience
- Leads to separation of the soul and lack of fulfillment
- Stems from lack of self-love

Forgiveness
- Forgiveness is important when expectations have gone unmet.

- Acceptance of yourself will lead you to being nonjudgmental of others.
- You, and only you, are responsible for yourself.

Technological modalities to enhance spiritual growth
- Accelerate multidimensional expressions
- Sound vibrations/tonal qualities
- Color
- Vision
- Any modality that enhances awareness of all the senses to promote a higher vibrational frequency
- Can assist in entraining the brain to recognize higher states of consciousness.

The Trinity/Triad
- Mother/father/child external and internal expressions

Chapter 6

Angels and Spirit Guides

"The unseen assistance of beings present for all to experience in the asking when the heart is open to receiving. They impact one's life in the knowing that one is not alone and can be touched by God."
—THEO

It was reported in a recent poll that 78 percent of us believe in angels. This is not surprising in light of the significant amount of media attention given to the subject over the past several years. The number of reported angelic contacts and lifesaving interventions is remarkable. All things supernatural, including miracles, guardian angels, life after death, spiritual mediumship, channeling, and so on, have been the subjects of television and radio shows, books, movies, magazines, and Web sites.

As we experience an accelerated opening to these topics, it is certain that our interest in these areas will grow. Every radio show and public THEO experience that we host evoke personal accounts of experiences with nonphysical entities. As the participants receive confirmation and guidance from THEO about their health or relationships, or communicate with a deceased loved one, it becomes clear that we are in the presence of angels—whether we believe it now, or in a few months.

Most of us have had, or know someone who has had, an unexplainable experience. This kind of personal interaction with "the other side" can be most confirming and most exciting, or frightening, depending on your perception. Angels, spirit guides, energies, entities, ghosts—however you would perceive them—interact with humanity in a variety of ways. Meditation creates a highly receptive state for contact with these beings and for receiving messages and guidance from them. The moments prior to falling asleep, and the dream state are also ideal times for this communication.

These angelic beings also communicate with us in our normal waking state and exhibit humor and playfulness. For example, in the summer of 1998 we were driving through Michigan, talking and listening to an oldies radio station and, in general, enjoying each other's company, when suddenly the music on the radio began to play at full volume. Of course, each of us thought that the other, for some unknown reason, had turned up the dial. The dial itself *bad* been turned up physically, but neither of us had touched it. Then, as we turned down the volume control, we noticed that the song that was playing was "These Magic Moments." And, as if to be sure that we would not pass this experience off as mere coincidence, the next song, played without commercial break, was "Do You Believe in Magic." We questioned THEO about the experience after returning to Phoenix. THEO reported that they, too, thoroughly enjoyed the interaction.

We encourage you to invite your angelic friends into your life and create some magic of your own. For, in addition to providing you with life-enhancing guidance, they will also make your life more interesting.

How do you, as twelve Archangels, retrieve information that you pass on to us?

We are aware in that sense of working with individuals. We engage in their energetic field, their soul field as well, to inform, to become aware of their intent of that which is their life experience, of that which has been their past. It is as one would perceive, as many have spoken in the past, of the Akashic records but that would be in your present day the model of your computer. We have the ability to come into an environment vibrationally that is the soul, to be aware of its full essence.

Speak more to coming into that environment.

In essence we blend with the soul to be fully aware of the being.

The soul has all memory of all lifetimes, all experiences in and out of the physical, is that correct?

Yes.

Does it just take those experiences with it that it needs for its growth, those that would be most profound, or most important?

Those that are most influential in that present engagement, let us say, yes.

Are you a manifestation of the Holy Spirit?

We are. Yes. We are the messengers of God. We are, as you are, the Holy Spirit. We are that which is a connectedness to God, which is the Holy Spirit. So in that questioning, we are, as well as you. You are a full embodiment or manifestation of that spirit.

That spark of God?

Yes.

What is an angel?

An angel is that which would be a presence or a soul, embodied or out of body, that is a direct messenger or guide of the God source, to facilitate and assist humanity.

Why have angels become so popular in the last several years?

That is because you are experiencing them and accepting them in your higher conscious states; awareness of other dimensional experiences, other dimensions, other beings, should we say, in other dimensions as well. There is fuller awareness that one is not only the physical structure but beyond that, and that the earth is not only one experience but there are other dimensions in which to experience. So their beliefs have changed. The expansion of consciousness has allowed for personal experiences that confirm this, so there is a greater interest because there is a recognition that it is possible. There is a well-documented story for humanity that was a true experience of a sailing ship that anchored in a harbor. The indigenous people were unaware of what a sailing ship was, and did not even see it until one day one of the people became more aware and looked into the harbor and saw the ship there, then brought it to the attention of the others. So this is part of what has happened to your experience as human beings. There has been an evolution of consciousness, of awareness, to have personal experiences and know that these are true. Fully aware. And so as beings experience, touch, know to be true, it is brought to the forefront.

What is the difference between an angel and a spirit guide? Or are they one and the same?

There are differences in angelic legions and there are differences in angels. There are those of the hierarchy that have not been embodied in the physical structure of humankind. There are those that are angelic beings that have incarnated into a physical structure; so there are different legions of angels numbering in the hundreds of thousands and millions; so there is that which have specific jobs to do with humanity and in specific jobs in other dimensions. So it is, the conscious mind has not the vision to perceive all that there is.

Why is it that we are usually unable to see angels? Is their vibrational frequency too high and ours too dense?

For the most part, it is not necessary for angelic beings to adjust the frequency so that they can be seen. It is true that the frequency is a very high vibration that the eye cannot see. However, as you know in personal experiences of some beings upon visions, they can be seen, as can the masters.

As amazing as those experiences are, they are still few and far between. What determines the frequency of these types of experiences?

Need.

Confirmation?

Confirmation, yes. Acceptance, yes. It would be dependent upon the circumstance.

How are spirit guides connected to what several different spiritual teachers refer to as our higher self.

It is that full soul awareness. There is a higher self that has full knowledge and connectedness. There is some education to the self by this remembering. However, as to guides and mentors, these are teachers and we can relate it back to your educational system. When one is in a particular learning modality, there are particular teachers for that. As one learns those lessons of that particular teacher, then one graduates from that classroom and goes on to the next of choosing. Then there are other teachers with that wisdom and that information for the student, and then a graduation and a going on to the next. So guides and mentors, or teachers, change as the being evolves and moves through those lessons that have been chosen. As to angelic guardians, these stay constant with the individual throughout a lifetime.

Is there some soul agreement with our guardian angel prior to us incarnating?

There is agreement, yes.

I know that we have no conscious picture or remembrance, yet, of just how this all really works, but it would seem as though it would be a really boring job to just hang out with one human being for a whole lifetime.

Not necessarily, for angels learn the human experience by interacting with humans, with beings, with souls, that have chosen the human experience. So there is an exchange.

Would guardian angels be beings that, in fact, have a soul as we do and may have been incarnated in the past?

Possibly, yes. Not always.

Can you speak to the angelic hierarchy?

There are many legions of angels, seraphim, cherubim, virtues, different legions holding tens of thousands of angels, assisting being particular to one dimension or another, or to earth, or to guardianship, whatever it might be. Then there are those that one perceives as managers or leaders in these legions, in particular pods, one might think it, or classes, or however one could perceive structure. Archangels are those that are overseers and leaders of these legions; they are connected to the God source. If one is in the military one could think of God as the ultimate leader and the archangels as the generals. And then there would be mentors or leaders that would be then on down through the lineage or hierarchy to assist and direct and facilitate and oversee others. Not all are working in the earthly environment with individuals. Some are in other dimensional experiences. The mind has not the full awareness of what that could be, for there is not a picture of it in the head.

Is there such a thing as the Devil?

One could be created. What one perceives as the devil is an entity that victimizes humanity. It is that which are positive and negative energies, and there are those that react and act out negative energies, that then would perceive the devil as influential within that, for it is escape. For if one perceives the devil making them victimized or doing something, then one relinquishes their own personal power, do they not? Or one could perceive that God was making them good. Who is really making them good? They are. To relinquish one's power is inappropriate action in any circumstance. Ask for assistance, yes. Ask for a learning, for knowledge, for wisdom, yes. But to perceive that one usurps one's personal power to make them do anything is inappropriate and incorrect. Angelic beings have no power to usurp the free will of humankind. That which you speak of as the devil, or evil, is that which is innate in the human duality.

That which we create?

Yes.

What of Lucifer? Does he represent the negative, or evil, duality?

Lucifer is a leader of the virtues. Lucifer is not the angel of darkness as has been thought. Many lessons are learned by the virtues, for that depicts the name, does it not? It brings forth within the environment of human experience, the duality—the light, the dark, the positive the negative, but it is nothing but energy. One must see both sides, accept both sides, of personality, accept both energies, both polarities, and when one accepts both polarities of the being, one comes into balance, and fulfillment. So when one recognizes Lucifer as being lesser than, that is not so. Lucifer is a great teacher.

Would the teachings about Lucifer be more from humans creating Lucifer in the image of something evil or dark—the devil.

Fear is why humans have placed Lucifer as the dark, and one perceives dark as bad or negative. It is not so. There is great beauty in the darkness.

Is it all pure love in the higher dimensions?

It is love, yes. For you see, when there is total awareness, there is acceptance, is there not? Enlightenment.

How do we get in touch with our angels?

Meditational process allows for one to be in more direct contact. But in the asking there can be contact. In the asking there is receptivity.

This would answer then why some people have contact and others do not. If I am hearing you correctly, everybody who asks will have contact.

Yes, but then there would be those who would say that I have asked and asked and have not contacted or felt contacted. In the asking one must be open to receive. In learning receptivity and allowance, it cannot only be asking, and when one comes to the door have it shut. So one could ask and ask, but if one truly is not open to receiving guidance, acceptance, what they are asking for, then nothing can penetrate that shield. And know that sometimes in the asking, the answer is no, for it is not of the highest good, in whatever may be asked for.

But that would seem contradictory to not usurping our free will. Who determines if it is in our highest good?

The soul. That is the highest will. There is something to be said for right timing. One may ask and ask and it may not be yet time for that outcome, or that process, or whatever it may be, for full acceptance, or full integration, or experience.

So there are some building blocks that the soul creates for us, one experience to the next?

Correct. There, too, is an evolutionary process.

How do we know if it is really a message from our guidance, or just something that we have created in our imagination?

As one goes forward in the asking and is open to receptivity there is information that is imparted, subtly at times and not so subtly at other times. And it is to recognize that not to try to judge where it comes from but more if it is working in one's life. It is not the messenger, it is the message. If it is from the higher self and it is workable, that is good. If it is from an angelic guide, this is good as well. One can know the difference by the confirmations in the external world.

That's all that really matters, isn't it?

Yes.

The form that it takes may be entirely different from that which we anticipated, doesn't it?

Yes, for the conscious mind can be limiting. It cannot know all things or perceive where the best outlet would be, or inlet.

So what is intuition?

Sensitivity ... to guidance, to path, to soul.

In a situation when we find ourselves in danger, and in need of protection, is it only in our asking that angels can work on our behalf? What if we don't ask and our life may be in danger?

That is why a guardian angel does become involved.

But again it gets back to the concept of not usurping free will. So if we are not aware of the guidance, and the opportunity to ask for that guidance, will that guidance be provided to us?

It would be. Most often that is part of the contract of a guardian.

So the soul would know it is not time to leave and the contract with the guardian would be enacted?

For assistance, yes.

What of the contacts made, or the experiences that people have without consciously requesting assistance or contact?

Most often when there is that assistance and there is a memory of it there has been an asking on some level, that there would be assistance at sometime, and a belief that that could be, in the depth of being. Not always is the assistance given at the time of the asking. In severe circumstances, yes. Note that there are those that pray and in their prayers they are asking. Matters not when they ask, necessarily.

Are we all angelic beings here in physical form?

One can choose this experience, yes. There are angelic hierarchical beings that have embodied in this time as teachers, to assist humanity. And their way of assisting, in the particular way that they are to assist, is to be embodied.

Many times we have witnessed remarkable spiritual healing of people who have spoken to their deceased loved ones through you. Based upon the information that you provide, there is no doubt that they are in communication with those souls. How are you able to access these souls for communication so quickly and easily?

Oftentimes they are very present about the individuals that are asking. We see them no differently than you. They are as present as you. So it is very easy to communicate with them when they are that present. There are times when they are not as present, and they are in other dimensional experiences when asked for. But because there is ultimately no time or space for us, we can make contact unless there is a decision on that soul's part to be in a learning modality that is not accessible at that time. You could think of it in terms, if you were in a business meeting and said, "I am not accessible at this time." Very similar.

What else can you add about becoming more receptive to contact with angels and spirit guides?

The meditative process on a regular daily basis allows one to be more fully receptive to all soul activity. It is a time of grand expansion and awareness of all that is seen, and unseen, of all the energy that permeates the earth experience and beyond. It is a grand expansion of consciousness. It is a grand experience for all—angelic beings, guides, mentors, and humans. Again, one is not greater than another. Each is a teacher and a student. Each is experiencing this grand expansion in their own way. Sharing the experience is blessed.

✣ *Reflections on Angels and Spirit Guides*

How do angels and spirit guides communicate?
- They vibrationally blend with your soul to become fully aware of your essence. It is an energetic connection.
- Your soul has the memory of all lifetimes, all experiences in and out of the physical body.
- Everyone is connected energetically as a unified energy field and aspect of God.

What is an angel?
- It is a direct messenger or guide from God that facilitates and assists humanity.
- An angel can be in agreement with a human being to assist exclusively for a period of time.

Why angels are so popular now
- Humanity is having more conscious experiences with these etheric beings.
- There is greater awareness of one being able to experience other dimensions.
- We have recognition of ourselves as more than our physical bodies.
- There are too many stories and accounts of angelic contacts to ignore or negate the reality of them.

Why we usually cannot see angels
- There are extremely high energetic frequencies that cannot be seen with human eyes.
- We can reduce vibration in certain circumstances to be seen when necessary.
- Angels will give confirmations in other ways as well.

How spirit guides are connected to the soul
- The full soul contains all knowledge and connectedness.
- Spirit guides communicate vibrationally to your higher self, which then transfers the messages to your conscious mind.
- As you evolve to higher consciousness, you will move on to other mentors and guides for additional learning.

Guardian angels
- Stay constant throughout your entire lifetime.
- Make soul agreement prior to incarnation.
- Learn the human experience by interacting with you.
- May have been incarnated in the past.

The angelic hierarchy
- God—ultimate leader Archangels—the overseers
- Many other legions particular to specific dimensions
  - Seraphim
  - Cherubim
  - Virtues
- The mind of human beings is limited in its perception of angelic entities.

Is there such a thing as the devil?
- Only if you create this entity to victimize yourself, to create an excuse for your own inappropriate actions.
- The "devil" doesn't make you do anything.
- Embrace the positive and negative aspects of yourself.
- By balancing the positive and negative energies, you will move into wholeness, fulfillment.
- To relinquish one's power is inappropriate action in any circumstance.

- What people perceive as the devil, or evil, is innate in the human duality. There is no reason to be fearful of the darkness, for you maintain your power by finding the beauty in it.
- Higher dimensions are pure love. Total awareness and acceptance equal enlightenment.

How to make contact with your angels and guides
- Meditate.
- Place intent; ask for communication.
- Be open to receive.
- Believe it will happen. Do not negate subtle experiences.
- Patience and recognition of perfect timing are necessary.
- Your soul determines what is in its highest good.

How to know if you are really receiving guidance
- Does it resonate as truth?
- Does it work for you in your life?
- Does it confirm that which you already felt you knew?
- Listen to the message. This is much more important than the messenger.
- Be open to the form that the guidance takes. It may be different than you think, for the conscious mind can be limiting.

Chapter 7

Multidimensional Experiences

". . . An awareness of one being more than the physical body."
—THEO

The recognition or remembrance of yourself as a multidimensional being is purely an experiential process, a process we don't have the words to describe. Occasionally we have asked THEO for clarification or confirmation regarding a particular experience only to be told that it is well to "experience the experience" without trying to define it with words. Moments of ecstasy, illumination, or at-one-ment represent movement to new heights of consciousness that the categorizing mind may interrupt with its tendencies. In these moments, when time and space collapse, the soul emerges. The undefined, wordless, sense-of-knowing received then stays with us. Forever. Later we may try to represent the experience in words, but we always fall short. Magic is that which happens beyond rationalization.

As we expand our perception to include multidimensional experiences, the old patterning of perceiving only with five senses begins to feel limiting. This shift of perspective creates an awareness that touches all aspects of our life and we may begin to view people and circumstances differently and we may begin to expect miracles and magic every day.

Experiencing multidimensional expressions of yourself can be scary and confusing. Many fear finding that they are as bad as they think they are; we fear losing control or venturing into unknown territory; we may think that the mind is like a very dangerous neighborhood: you don't want to go in there alone. The truth is that we begin to recognize the self as the grand spiritual being that it is. And we learn to trust it. As we invite multidimensional, multisensory experiences into our life, our soul will manifest only that which is for our highest learning. These experiences show up as our conscious mind becomes emotionally and psychologically receptive. We must be patient, however, and trust that these expressions will appear in our life; and meditate daily to increase our vibrational frequency and access to our spiritual awakening. For it is this high vibrational frequency that gives us access to spirit, to our soul.

THEO suggests that we pay attention to our dreams, to people and circumstances that show up in our life, to information and opportunities that suddenly appear, to what you see, hear, and feel while in meditation. Our soul will communicate with us in ways that we have not considered before. And have fun, for it is likely that we will develop our psychic abilities so fully that we will become authentic magicians, capable of living the miraculous moment-to-moment for the rest of our lives.

What does multidimensional experience mean?

It is that which is an awareness in the conscious state of experiences outside, or beyond, the body; it can be experienced within the body in that sense of a realization of that vibrational frequency being heightened, and being more in attunement to all energies that are about the self.

Can you speak more of these energies that are about the self?

Meaning that there are energies permeating the world's atmosphere in that which is the day-to-day existence. There are energies surrounding, there is dimensional energy that is available to the being to be conscious and aware of as one steps out of the time continuum, meaning that they go beyond, or collapse time and space, become aware of experiences that are happening all at once. One could perceive a dimensional collapse of time and space and an awareness of other dimensions as one might perceive a double-exposed photograph where there is one image upon another. Very similar, and that's a picture that the mind's eye could understand.

What does the term "holographic universe" mean?

Multifaceted. We speak of it in terms of a diamond with many facets, and as the light shines forth on one facet the light is refracted and that facet is seen. So it is very similar to this. As the light is shown, or the awareness is brought to one facet, or one dimension, then there is an awareness of it, or a cognition of it. We use that word because being cognitive of an experience is manyfold. Not only is it an understanding on the conscious level, but it is a physical experience as well.

We have had the experience, as have many others, of the collapse of time and space. What takes place when these collapses occur in our lives?

When one is fully present in an experience, there is no time. There is also the ability to transmit energy from one place to another, bilocating, as well that has been known about by some masters; that there is the ability to appear in two places at once, or that there would be no traveling time from one place to another.

How does that happen? How can we create that experience in our lives?

All beings have the ability to do that, but raising one's frequency to a high enough level to allow that to occur is what is necessary, and that can be done meditationally. A continuum of meditation raises the vibrational frequency to a high enough level that one then is aware that they can manipulate the molecular structure of the body, that they can either levitate or move from one place to another easily by thought.

And take the physical body with them?

Yes.

It sounds like we can create miracles or what we would perceive to be magic.

That is correct. There are what would be termed or deemed magicians that are showing that that can be. There are also those who have been meditating for years upon years upon years, developing the ability to raise one's frequency so that they would seem to disappear, or to levitate the body, raising the body without the muscular energy doing such.

Is this how Jesus was able to walk on water, by becoming weightless?

Yes.

So we have the ability to create these miracles and it is the meditative process coupled with placing the intent that allows this to occur?

The knowing, the belief. For if one does not believe it, one cannot do it.

What are the various energy bodies that actually are encompassed within and about our soul and our physical body?

There is the electric magnetic field or that which many would pursue by speaking in terms of auric field. It is an energy that is about the surface of the body that some can see, some cannot, many feel. It is what some call "in space" or "their space." All have experienced another coming into their energy field, their electric field, whether it be two feet away or six inches away, whatever it may be, there is an energetic feeling. The body will feel it physically. So all have experienced that. Know that that is the energy body that many work with when working with shifting polarities, and energy balancing. There is, of course, the physical structure. There is the spiritual body and the emotional body that lies closely to the physical body, and within it, specifically, in the brain, the mind, and the heart, being very centralized.

Speak more to that, please.

Those are the chakra areas that it is most felt—the heart area, and the head. The crown. All of them are interconnected. They all are part *of full* healthfulness. They all influence the physical structure.

Are all the nonphysical bodies that you have just spoken of encompassed within the soul?

The soul encompasses them, meaning the soul is a part of all of that.

Along those same lines, we hear many teachers speak about the different aspects of self, the basic self, the higher self, the subconscious self. Can you speak to the truth of the different selfs that we are and how they affect how we perceive and feel?

The higher self could be related to the soul. The intellectual self is that which is the problem solving of the brain in consciousness. The subconscious is another level of the brain that is addressed intuitively, it is addressed on the meditative level. It is also that aspect of the brain that functions the physicality. The consciousness is a small segment that is growing in its awareness, let us say, to other attributes that have been subconsciously utilized. Meaning that many of the things we have been speaking about in the sensory perceptive way are perceived in the subconscious and then brought forward into the consciousness. What is happening is an expansion of awareness and the consciousness side of the brain that allows for it to grow in awareness so that there is the utilizing more of the brain in a conscious way rather than in a subconscious way. And that is when beings are cognitive of experiences.

What is the difference between polarities and duality?

Polarities are energetics that maintain balance. There is a difference in that. Duality can be expressed in many ways, and particularly how it is expressed by us is that which is the positive or negative reactions.

That choice that we have in every circumstance in our life?

Yes, and a recognition of the positive/negative sides of personality, action and reaction.

So if I hear you correctly, there is no duality in other dimensions but there are polarities in other dimensions?

Correct. Polarities maintain balance. Equilibrium.

Would it be true that there are polarities in all the higher dimensions?

There are, for if not, they would be bumping into each other.

Speak more to that, please.

As there are planets in your universe, if there were no structure, there were not polarities, if there were not separations such as this, they would not be in their own integrity. Polarity is that which maintains the equilibrium or the balance. The duality is the expression and experiences of the different aspects of interaction. They can be spoken of and have been spoken of as polarities because they are opposite ends, they are opposite one unto the other. But if you speak of energetic polarity in the sense of balance, scientifically for the world, there is that necessity. If you are speaking of duality as a polarity, then that is a different meaning, is it not? Somewhat similar yet different.

How can people transmute the fear inherent in the unknown aspects of multidimensional expression, while manifesting experiences in a way that will provide for our highest spiritual growth?

First, we would speak to the fear. Fear within utilizing these multidimensional experiences comes forward from the intellect feeling out of control. That fear base is that one would lose control and surely they must die if there is a loss of this control. When one begins to experience multidimensional experiences, and it is confirmed that they would not die from lack of control, as it is pursued and found to be confirmed, that it is only an expanding awareness, then there is a greater comfort and expectation and enjoyment of the new adventure. How one can achieve these states, again it is repetitive, but the meditative aspect of the being allows one to begin to experience, to center within the self, to gain the confidence and to begin to open to experiences in a more gentle way of expression, and to take one step at a time. To feel the weightlessness of the meditation allows one then to experience other experiences, knowing full well that they would not lose the body, lose themselves, and that they are in control at all times. The greater fear is the loss of control.

You have spoken often of meditation as the catalyst for these experiences. In addition to meditation, what are some of the cutting-edge technologies and modalities that are currently available to us to help facilitate these experiences?

There are technologies in your present day that have been developed, particularly to be aware of the control of mind, or the control of the different levels of consciousness that humans have, and there are different technologies—biofeedback, there are hemi-sync sound vibrations. There are also metatones, which is the usage of one's voice manipulated in different octaves to raise the frequency and the balancing of the physical structure so that can occur. There are different modalities that can be utilized.

Are they modalities that quicken the process of spiritual awakening?

They can quicken it, yes.

Is there also a balancing or expansion in the portion of our brain that gets used as we integrate some of these technologies?

As it is experienced, as with any other expression in the physical, the more it is done, the more comfort there is in the consciousness, and the more capability and confirmation there is, there is more trust. Within any activity, there is greater success and a refinement of abilities.

We know that these experiences are fun, and that perceiving with a multisensory perspective is a very exciting way of living life, but what does this really have to do with the evolution of consciousness and our own spiritual growth?

When one has experiences in multidimensional expression, then one is fully aware that they are more than just a physicality and that they do have soul and spirit that is ongoing, and that this is one choice, not the be-all and end-all of experience, but one choice of experience for the time present.

We are observing that people are beginning to feel more comfortable sharing their experiences.

Yes, and as it is observed to be in the outer world experience, there is more communication, there is more seeking, there is more information imparted, there is an asking. For beings are here in this time to do this evolutionary consciousness shift. They are experiencing more of their totality and in doing such are seeking out confirmation and information that confirms and affirms to them their process.

In my own research experiencing the out-of-body state and other multidimensional experiences, it seems to be equally as much fun to bring the other dimensions to us as opposed to leaving our bodies to explore. Can you speak to that?

What is brought unto the self is a total awareness. Yes, that is correct.

Speak more to that, please.

That one needs not leave the physical body to experience but to be fully aware at all times of all capabilities. It is important to live fully in the embodiment that one has chosen, for the soul has chosen this time, this place to be embodied. To live within that body is extremely important, for the soul that has chosen to be embodied has chosen that for a particular purpose. For if it were not to be in this human body in an ongoing way, then there would be no purpose in incarnation.

Is there anything detrimental to that relationship, in having occasional out-of-body travel?

No. It is a confirmation that one is not limited to a physical body.

When people have out-of-body experiences, what is the separation that takes place, and how do we remain attached to our physical body?

There is a common cord of attachment to the physical structure, much like an umbilical cord attached to the mother when the child is in utero. When consciousness or the soul leaves the physical structure, it is only for moments at a time even though it may seem that it is longer than that. For when the soul is out of the body, there is a timelessness, it is dimensional at that point, not linear. However, that soul is fully aware that it is to be in the body and that at any time can replace itself into that physical container, so there would not be a loss. As beings experience being in and out of the body, it confirms that there is a soul to the self. One then begins to see that one has full free will, meaning that if one wishes to be out of the body, it is out of the body, if one wishes to be in the body, it is in the body. And that is a choice.

Are we beginning to live heaven on earth as the veils are being lifted between the dimensions?

Yes, that is a realization that there is multidimensional experience and what comes about in living of heaven on earth is a realization and acceptance of one's totality, and then there is great joy. So when one is on earth or in heaven, they would feel the totality of love in all experiences.

Sheila and I have had experiences of being in and out of each other's energy fields, merging our energies while in meditation. We could be thousands of miles apart when this happens. Could you explain this energy exchange between two people?

It is telepathic; it is sending the energy back and forth. It is an awareness of the collapsing of time and space. It is as the energy of electricity: it is in the air, it is unseen, but can be experienced. Think in terms of that energetic microwave.

How can we manifest these experiences?

It is the intention that is important. Intend it and then when it is acceptable, psychologically and emotionally, and there is an openness to it, it will happen spontaneously. It is not forcing. Forcing only means that it is intellectually aligned— and it cannot be done intellectually, it must be done from the heart to the head, not the head to the heart.

Is this the "cocreation" you speak of? Or is cocreation between our soul and the divine will of our Creator?

There are many forms of cocreation, are there not?

Speak to that, please.

One can cocreate with another, an event. When you speak of cocreation one must define what it is.

Cocreate our experience. Cocreate finding our life purpose.

The soul creates a blueprint, let us say, to build upon in a particular incarnation. The soul then cocreates energetically with the human expression for that outcome, for the conscious mind.

That is the higher power. That is the divine aspect of this cocreation, correct?

It is.

It is the aspect of God that we create with, that being our soul.

Correct.

What of taking our physical bodies out of this dimension into other dimensions. Some people refer to this as ascension. Is this possible now, and is this something we can even benefit from?

Taking the physical body with the consciousness? Many masters have done that, and yes, there is a capability to it.

What would the benefit to us be in doing that?

It is a manifestation that one can achieve and is again having to do with heightened frequency. Making the frequency so high that the molecular structure dissolves, so to speak, the encasement, and then can be brought back together at will. But unless one has the experience, there is not the full understanding of it.

I would imagine that would be somewhat astonishing the first time it happens.

If you are of the awareness and the abilities to do it, it is not. And there have been accounts of this documented. Each being is a master and has the capability, but it is not the purpose at all times for each individual.

It seems as though we fail to remember the majority of our multidimensional experiences, particularly those that take place in the dream state. Are we moving into a time of more remembrance now with these experiences, and with more conscious control?

Yes. That is correct.

What takes place when we have very lucid dreams that include our deceased loved ones? How is it that they end up in our dreams?

You end up in their environment, they don't end up in yours. The soul, the being that is dreaming so to speak, leaves the body and engages with them. For they are present in the other dimensions and so the being engages in another dimensional experience.

These experiences are remarkable. They feel very real. Is it about placing intent to create this?

There is an asking on a soul level. It allows them to witness in their own experience the abilities that one has through their own personal experience and knowing a trust evolves for growth of consciousness and awareness.

What aspect of our being, or our soul, leaves the physical form to go into that multidimensional experience in those lucid dreams?

The soul. Fully.

What is the difference between an out-of-body experience and a lucid dream which would take place without the clear remembrance of the separation from the physical body?

A lucid dream is an awareness of the information that the mind is trying to impart as it is imparting it. There is a consciousness that occurs in the mind out of desire for clarity, the intent of learning. For lucid dreams are informational, often symbolically so, and at times very literal. So it is a way of discernment of one's growth or process, should we say.

Can it be accurately interpreted that we are making a connection with our soul, the highest aspect of ourselves?

The consciousness is making a connection with the soul, yes. And different fragmented parts of the soul will communicate in this way.

Speak more to that, please.

There can be a communication of the fragmented parts of the soul in a lucid dream to gain information to particular circumstances that created the patterning in one's life at present. That is what lucid dreams can do. They also can be prophetic.

So when we dream, is it our soul in all of our dreams? Is it our soul that leaves and has that experience?

When it is that type of a dream.

What of those dreams that are just bizarre and nightmarish, or vague and difficult to remember?

Oftentimes it is the conscious brain, or the brain, alleviating stimulus from the day-to-day life that it has absorbed.

A clearing away, so to speak?

Yes, deleting. This is a good word, is it not? It is a vernacular that has begun to be utilized and understood throughout humanity, and a greater understanding because of your machinery of how the soul works. It is an outward expression you see. Hmm, we find this amusing.

My personal angelic contacts and out-of-body experiences have been preceded by what is described as the "night paralysis." What is this state and why does it occur?

It feels as if it is a paralysis, but the soul raises above the body and, when the body is not connected to the soul, then it does not have the capability to work fully. It maintains its function because the brain is there as the main system, having the heart beating, all of the muscles working, all of these things, but the soul rises out of the body and then it is an object not fully functioning.

Yet often my consciousness remains in my physical body.

Your awakened consciousness, yes.

Does the consciousness not travel with the soul? Is there a separation?

There is a bit of a separation or it feels as if it is separate. There are times when the consciousness leaves the body as well, and there is not a memory, as you know.

Is there learning taking place on a deeper level that will be accessed at a later time?

Yes.

What happens when we have dreams or premonitions that turn out to be true? Often they are not very pleasant experiences, such as premonitions of loved ones dying.

It is preparatory. When there is a premonition, or an awareness of that which is to come, oftentimes, most often, it is either first to confirm that it is a capability. The other is preparatory. It prepares the being psychologically and physically for what is to come. And there is no time. It is also a confirmation of that. That one has tapped into another dimension of experience that, it is at the same time, collapsing time and space, so to speak.

There is a lot of that taking place today, isn't there?

Yes.

Why now? Is it just the time we live in, the vibrational frequency that we can now access?

Yes. Awareness. Readiness. Acceptance. All of these things for human evolution of consciousness.

We have had experiences that can only be described as telepathy. Being able to telepathically communicate with one another. What takes place energetically when we communicate that way?

Focus. Exchange of vibrational frequency. Very similar to the frequencies that surround you, that are a part of your electricity. Think of it as electricity.

Are there places known to be highly charged energetically on the planet where we can experience a higher vibration and, perhaps, have a portal open to other dimensions or other worlds?

There are energy vortexes throughout the earth expression, yes, particularly in mountainous regions there are high vortexes. There can be vortexes within the water So we could speak specifically of very different ones and different states and different countries, but all countries have them and all places within a few miles of one another, in actuality. So there is just not few in number, there are great numbers of energy vortexes about the earth.

What is an energy vortex?

It is a pulsation of energy that permeates through the earth or reflects from the universe, let us say. It can be reflective or a drawing.

Speak more to that, please.

There are two polarities, are there not; repelling and attracting? That is what we are speaking about. The vortexes, the energy, can be felt upon the land. Many would perceive that in those vortexes they receive and experience the soul better, or experience a collapse in time and space. In a vortex there is a heightened frequency which does allow one sensitized to experience more multidimensional experiences.

When you speak of water, it brings up the question of the Bermuda Triangle and the planes and ships that were lost in that part of the world. Can you speak to what happened there?

Attraction. A polarity that is attraction; magnetic; drawing in. One might perceive it as a black hole as many have observed on the earth, or a sinking.

So what happened to those planes and those ships that were lost in that area, and the people that were on them?

Many would like to think that they went to the other side of the earth into something else or into the internal of the earth. Not so. That which disappeared the molecular structure dissolved. The beings as well. It is that high intensity.

So the physical beings died?

Correct.

And the planes and boats just disappeared?

Yes.

What of the building of the great pyramids, which is thought by some to have been a multidimensional project?

To some extent it was. Those that did the architectural design were of high vibrational frequency, were very high souls.

In physical forms?

In physical forms. They embodied and engaged those beings who built them with the proper abilities to bring it forth, meaning the knowledge of how to place the stones. The knowledge of how to transport the stones with greater ease. The energy conducted within these pyramids is very strong. That design or the geometries of it came from souls of high beings.

But built entirely by human beings?

They were. The humans were given the tools to do it, meaning the abilities.

What else can you add regarding multidimensional experiences and their role in our lives now?

Many have thought of them as something outside themselves and it is very much an internal process. That which engages the full soul integration allows for the being to be fully capable of experiencing the timelessness or other dimensions, not limited to this physical structure in its linear way, but open and receptive to all there is to experience. So that is the time that you are moving into. It is that fuller awareness of the spiritual beingness of self that is no longer limited linearly, and can bring forth and experience many things of great wonder that brings about the ability to fully love the self. That is a blessing. For through these experiences gains a trust within the conscious mind of man that then can be expressed more fully with the totality of acceptance, the integration unto soul, and the love of the self.

✤ *Reflections on Multidimensional Experiences*

Definition of multidimensional experience
- An awareness of being more than the physical body
- Being in attunement to all the energies about the self
- Collapse of time and space
- Can be perceived as a double-exposed photograph
- Like a diamond with many facets with the light shining through

Collapsing time and space
- Being fully present in the experience
- Can transmit energy from one place to another
- No travel time from one place to another
- Must raise vibrational frequency to manipulate the molecular structure of the body
- Creates magic, miracles
- Must place intent and believe it can be

The energy bodies encompassed within and about the physical body
- Electromagnetic field—auric field
- Spiritual body
- Emotional body

The aspects of self
- Higher self—soul
- Intellectual self—the problem solving of the brain in consciousness
- Subconscious self—addressed intuitively on a meditative level. The aspect of the brain that functions the physicality.
- Consciousness—a small segment that is growing in awareness to other attributes that have been subconsciously utilized

Polarities and duality

Polarities are energetics that maintain equilibrium, balance. Duality can be expressed as that which is positive and negative reactions. A recognition of positive and negative sides of personality. Action and reaction. Choice.

- Polarities exist energetically in other dimensions— duality is specific to the human experience.
- Polarities maintain energetic integrity.

Transmuting fear of the unknown aspects of multidimensional experiences

- Observe that the intellect fears being out of control.
- Know that you will not die and you ultimately are in control. Take it one step at a time.
- Each experience brings greater comfort, expectation, and joy to the adventure of self-discovery.
- The weightlessness felt in meditation gently opens the door to other experiences.

Technologies that assist in facilitating multidimensional experiences

- Biofeedback
- Hemi-Sync sound vibrations—metatones

Out-of-body experiences

- Recognition of ourselves as more than physical bodies, acknowledgment of our souls
- Not necessary to bring in the awareness and information from the higher dimensions (can be done in-body)
- Physical body remaining attached to the soul through an energetic chord
- A timeless experience not limited by linear time
- Safe, the soul always returning to the physical body
- Intention and openness to the experience necessary for manifestation

- Happens spontaneously when it is acceptable psychologically and emotionally
- Must be done from the heart to the head, not the head to the heart
- First, "night paralysis," the soul leaving the body, and the body then unable to move

Communicating with deceased loved ones
- Often they are present with those asking.
- Ultimately there is no time or space, which our conscious minds cannot fully understand.
- Our souls enter other dimensions when we meet during lucid dreaming.

Lucid dreaming
- The soul has the experience.
- Pay close attention to them, for there are many messages.
- Premonitions will prepare you psychologically and physically for what is to come: they represent collapse of time and space.

Telepathic communication
- Exchange of vibrational frequency
- Can be thought of as electricity

Planetary energy vortexes
- Mountainous regions are often high frequencies.
- There are vortexes within the water.
- A vortex is a pulsation of energy that permeates through the earth or reflects from the universe, and can be reflective or attracting.

Chapter 8

Manifestation

"The power of the word and of the thought is the creative force."
THEO

Since 1985, THEO has been teaching humanity that it is shifting energetically into the 5th Dimension. They describe this planetary energy as a spiritual frequency that exalts us to express ourselves as more than physical bodies. Inherent in this remembrance of ourselves as spiritual beings is the activation of magnificent abilities beyond the limitations of five sensory perceiving.

You have a choice to believe that you can create miracles in your life or not. It is our experience that the tools given us by THEO are very effective, and the perception that something miraculous can happen at any moment in our lives has made life more fun. In our personal and professional lives the confirmations are continuous as people, information, money, answers, and other expressions show up at the perfect time. We know that a large part of being able to manifest these experiences comes from the belief that we will. It requires only a shift in perception.

The universal energy of creation works in wondrous ways. It is our job to "get in the flow of it" if we want it to work for us in manifesting all of our dreams and desires. Imagine a sailboat at the moment the wind fully catches the sails propelling it forward effortlessly, with you at the tiller, making minor adjustments as needed.

In the interest of manifesting your dreams and hopes, we would like to share with you one way that we manifest ours: Write down on paper that which you desire and place that piece of paper in a special container or box. We call our "The God Box." It can be an unused jewelry box, a small wooden box, or in anything that has some special meaning to you. You may check on it periodically, as you like. We revisit our "God Box" once a year on our birthdays (They are one day apart) and celebrate as we recognize how many of our dreams have come true during the past year.

Now that we are in the fifth dimensional energy, how does this affect our ability to manifest our desires?

It is a refinement of energy. It is the abilities, an awareness; a consciousness for humanity now that they have full ability to think, to project, to accept and to receive that which would be their desire fully. There's also an awareness, in this energetic time, that there is that capability, and that the thought processes are the creative force, for many are experiencing this manifestation process now.

Is our ability to manifest dramatically greater now than it has been in any other time in history?

There has always been ability, however, there is a consciousness that one has that ability so that in the consciousness there's a greater receptivity. It is also a refinement of energy that allows for that to be more fully experienced, let us say. So, in essence, yes, it is far easier for this to occur – less resistance.

Can you explain the process that makes thought the creative force?

It is creativity, it is an energy exchange. It is that which is the thought perceiving; it is perceptivity. Do you understand? That then allows one to formulate, let us say, matter. If one desires a chair, then one perceives it first, do they not? So it is perceptivity, as well as projection. You wish us to speak of the physiological or the physics of the circumstance that is the creation, and we have no words that would allow for the head to understand, nor for the masses to perceive. A scientific mind could do such but the masses could not in general. Do you understand? It is experiential. The projection of thought, then the occurrence in one's life. Many can do this in the sense of individuals placing intent on another, have one call them up. Many can do this in the sense of individual placing intent on another, having one call them up. So there is that telepathic occurrence. As one begins to perceive that they can think about something and then receive it, drawing it to them, magnetizing it. Manifestation is only magnetizing, becoming a magnet to that which you wish and desire.

So, we're talking about the law of attraction, correct?

You are.

Please explain the process involved.

It is a process. It is experiential. To do it is the confirmation. To do it and to have the experience of it being completed, and the attraction or the manifestation then occurring. Then as one experiences and attempts again and has confirmation of it happening, then it becomes an occurrence that is continual. When things are experiential, it is difficult to describe in words, for the words are limiting to the experience. Do you understand? We wish people not to be caught up in the words but to enjoy and to experience the experience.

What's the relationship between neurolinguistic programming and the manifestation process that you are describing?

It is beliefs about particular words. That's what we're saying, that words can be limiting. So in the neurolinguistic programming, it is to shift words particularly that block the flow in one's life circumstance. For each individual has particular words that are uncomfortable because they have been used in a negative way in their environment. It is not the word that has the energy, it is the energy placed upon the neurolinguistic programming, it is training and entraining the mind and the brain and the being to use words that are attractive rather than repelling. Meaning, if there is a word that is uncomfortable for a personality, it can attract a negative because of their belief or the feeling they have about that particular word. So it is retraining the self to use words that are attractive, similar in content, but less charged in a negative way. For many of the words that block, block because of a lack of self-esteem attached to them, an unworthiness that is felt.

What are some of the tools that you can provide us for manifestation?

When there is a desire, there is a creation of a thought that is a bridge to that outcome. So when one has a thought or a desire to be manifested, one then creates the thought bridge, meaning those attitudes and perceptions that are positive for that outcome. That places that bridge of thought into the universe for that manifestation to occur. There is a universal energy that is the attraction or creative energy that when one places the thought, or the seed, let us say, as if in one's garden, places a seed, then it creates an environment of gestation that then allows for the growth of that seed to become a flower. So what you are doing with your thought is placing the seed, on the intention, in the fertile soil. The universal energies is the soil in which it is placed ultimately, and the intent and the thought and the positive actions or thoughts is that which is the food to fertilize and feed the seed to bring it to fruition. In turn it is also that which is the attraction, the energy attraction to that positive outcome. Not to negate it with a negative thought, that it could not be so, because that breaks down the bridge to the universal energy that attracts.

Then it is critical to move from the place of questioning our self-worth into a place of self-love, which if I am hearing you correctly, is really at the core of this whole process.

Knowing that one is worthy of all that they desire. But then one must be judicious in their desires for surely they will manifest. Be certain it is what you want. So then one becomes discerning of those desires, gains clarity within the self of what one truly wishes. In that certainty and awareness of self and thought process then one lives the life to its highest good, do they not? Then one wastes not their energy on the unimportant but on that which would be the joyfulness and bliss that they seek and desire.

What determines the length of time that it takes for us to manifest certain desires?

Openness and receptivity, and living into that receptivity. Oftentimes it takes some growth on the part of the individual, or if others are involved, a combined growth of acceptance. Do you understand? Timing, right timing is one's evolutionary process. And the soul defines that, not the conscious human being.

How can we most effectively manifest financial abundance in our lives?

First, by addressing the old belief systems that one is not worthy of the abundance that one seeks. And know that can come from family structure, most often does, from the patternings within the structure of family that have been learned. As one's soul enters the body it is in full awareness of its uniqueness perfection and divinity and there is a belief that it does deserve all that it desires. Not from an egocentric point of view, but from a centered self, a soulful self. But as it enters into a physical structure it does adopt and become like those environments in which it is living. The conscious mind adheres to beliefs and patternings that it is taught. So as one desires financial abundance, one must look within the self to that ability to receive, to relinquish those old patterns that do not serve that outcome, and to recognize the worthiness of the being for an abundant life on all levels, not only financial but all of that which is part of the earthly experience.

Does the purpose that accompanies the desire to make lots of money have anything to do with our ability to manifest it? Some people would have the intent of sharing it with the world and for the highest good of all people, others for their own selfish reasons. Does this intent matter?

No.

So, there's no judgment about that?

There is not. More importantly, good deeds are good deeds, they stand unto themselves. Greed and egotism stand for itself as well. For the intention of the soul is to grow and to learn and to experience. Each experience is manifested unto the self for that process, do you understand, whatever that learning may be, whatever that feeling may be, whatever the emotion is. One cannot judge another's experience, for the soul will manifest perfectly what is appropriate for its growth.

There are those on a spiritual path who have had the perception that financial abundance is somehow contradictory to spirituality. This is not true, is it?

It is not true. Many have stated that God judges those with abundant lives. It's God's desire, if you would, for all beings to have abundant lives. That is the birthright. It is an experience that can be achieved. But not from that egotistical point of view, but as one goes forward and recognizes that one is worthy of an abundant life, whatever that might be, each being has their own perception of what it is, you. But ultimately what humanity seeks, and we are speaking in generality now, is happiness, and peacefulness in heart. Finances, money, cannot achieve that alone, do you understand – most often does not. For money, in and of itself, has no energy. It is what humanity places on it, the energetic that gives it its power. Perception, is it not? It is a tool. It is only a tool of learning, of process. And, of course, when you live in an environment where there is this exchange, it has created an energetic exchange, the energy is placed on it, you see. And ones exchange it, one unto the other for services and for food, for sustenance, and for shelter, do they not? There can be equal energetic exchanges, for that it needs not be money. But in your environment that is what it has become an energetic exchange.

How do we manifest spiritually fulfilling romantic relationships?

By becoming romantic within the self. Meaning, when one is fully aligned with the self, and integrated with the self, and self-loving, then it is made manifest in the outer world experience. Then it is allowed the vulnerability, because on is whole within self, without the expectation of another creating that wholeness. Then one is fulfilled inwardly and can express fulfillment out into the world and attract that unto the self on all levels – romantic, sexually, financially. One then knows how to receive. For many think giving is the lesson, no, the greater lesson is receptivity. Being able to receive is the greater lesson.

Why is it so difficult for us to receive?

The belief of not being good enough or worthy enough. It is a belief, it is a perception, a judgment of the self.

Could you address the relationship between the doing and the allowing aspects of manifesting?

Allowing is having a waiting, a period of time when there is a comfortableness in waiting for opportunity to present itself, and the doing then can be. As many have found in doing, doing, doing, it does not allow for receptivity. It is an expenditure of energy that has no allowance. So it is more important to place intent and desire out, and to learn the patience and the awareness as opportunities present; to discern and then to act. It is better use of energy, is it not?

Are there no limits to what we are capable of manifesting and will we be able to manifest instantly that which we desire?

Yes. And many are experiencing, as they move forward in the acceptance of one's totality and integration into the whole self, the ability to manifest in the immediate all their wishes and desires. Meaning that there are beings that have the ability and awareness, that place intent and act upon the energy as it is brought forward, and have the trust in the manifestational process. So it would then be perceived as instant manifestation, for there are no blockages. There is the placing of the energy forward, the intent, the thought, and then the reflection in the immediate back to the outcome or the event. Do you understand? For then there is the collapse of time and space, and that is the immediate. So there would be the placed intention, and the receptivity, and the awareness of it. That is in the millennium to come. It is in the present.

Will we be able to manifest, as some people on this planet are known to do, whatever it would be that they would desire at that time?

This is what many people perceive as magic.

Exactly. And so the question we get asked often is, how do we really learn how to do that? Is it a learned ability or is it a remembered ability that we simply allow ourselves to be open to?

It is allowance. The ability is there. It is a remembrance, it is an allowance, it is a recognition, it is a trust, it is a perception. All of those things come into play within that…and knowing.

Is there any guidance outside of ourselves that influences this process?

There is much guidance outside the self when requested.

In the manifestation process, is that applicable?

Assistance?

Yes. Or is it entirely from within ourselves that we are able to manifest?

When asked, there is assistance. But it is within the self that the asking comes, does it not? So the answer is yes on both counts.

How do past life experiences affect our ability to manifest in this life?

Out of old patterns and beliefs of not being good enough. That is why it is a time of full soul integration. For there are those fragmented parts of the soul that do influence the patternings of beliefs within this incarnation. Soul integration. Do you see?

Along those same lines, do we, in fact, create in our reality that which we fear the most?

For is that not a thought? Yes.

There is no differentiation, is there?

There is not. And there is no judgment.

So, if we are fearful of something and attach any energy to that fear, it is likely we will manifest that in our lives, isn't it?

Yes. Energy does not define what is projected. The energy does not judge or define the projection of thought. It is an energy that is placed forward, whether it be a fear energy or that which one might term positive. Do you understand? There is only energy. And the universal experience is that it is then mirrored back unto the self. Do you understand? Whatever, it is that energy. So the universal energies do not define if one places a fear base for creation, or the desire for money as the creation, it does not discern or judge it. There is no capability of that, you see? Energy is energy. That is why we stated be judicious in your desires, be discerning in your desires, for surely they will manifest. And a desire can be fearfully based.

Do we create traumatic events such as rape or horrible injuries or abuses through our thoughts and words? Do we draw these into our experience?

Through a belief. Yes.

The belief that they may happen?

The fear. Again, that's energy. And it is a projection of thought. It is also that it is a bit more complex than that. It is simplistically stated as we have. But the questioning would be why would an infant be abused? But know that is a soul lesson and oftentimes for the adult or the parent, not only the child. The soul chooses perfectly what is important for its growth. The soul has a blueprint of experiences. Know that oftentimes, particularly in an infant or a young being, a young body, the soul is very old and wise and comes in as a teacher for that body or that environment – those personalities that it touches, whether it be individuals or society. It could have a broader teaching or a very singularly purposed teaching. There are many martyrs that have been in the work, have there not?

So when we place a thought on a particular desire, and an opposing force, another human being or group of human beings, has an opposite intent, what determines the outcome of that?

As to the question being, can another block the manifestation for another, ultimately no. Unless the personality that is placing the intent has a belief that the can do it. For it is the individual belief that is important here. It would be whoever would be most powerful in their intent, and their belief of its outcome. So if you have ten personalities and an equal ten on the other side, and all remain focused on the exact same outcome, each will create a different event, would they not? If it is a similar event, and one wants to usurp the will of the other, to be more powerful, then all things being equal, if there is one in the ten that has a belief that it could not happen, that weakens its structure, does it not? So in a weakened structure, the outcome can be changed yes.

And the more people involved in a particular desire for a particular manifestation, the more likely that the event will happen as desired.

Yes. Power in numbers.

As we wrap up this chapter, what else can you share with us about manifestation?

It is God's desire that all beings have the abundance that they seek. It is important in the individual, within the environment of the earth, to understand that it is the ultimate love that allows beings to manifest all they desire. It is the ultimate love that allows beings not to manifest all that they desire, for therein lies the lessons. Love the self. Fully integrate the self, and all things are possible.

✤ *Reflections on Manifestation*

We are now living in the 5ᵗʰ Dimension

- Higher frequency and refinement of planetary energies
- Positively affected by planetary alignments
- No coincidence that it is happening now, 2000 years after the time of Christ
- Greater receptivity and less resistance now than in any other time in the history of our planet

Tools for manifestation

- Building the thought bridge
- Do not negate with a negative thought that it cannot be so
- Planting of the seed into the soil of universal energy which is an environment of gestation
- Love yourself and feel worthy of receiving all you desire
- Eliminate old patterns leading to low self-esteem and of not feeling deserving enough
- Be discerning in your desires
- Write down your desires

Look for confirmations and answers in all aspects of your life

- Dreams
- Meditations
- Telepathic communications – thinking of someone and having them call almost immediately
- Personal meetings. Look for purpose in all activities
- Money or other needs being met just when you needed them to be

Neurolinguistic programming
- It is not the word that has the energy but the energy that is placed upon the word
- The belief associated with the word creates the outcome
- Retrain your thinking to free blockages and to use words that are attractive to you

Length of time it takes to manifest
- Not always when or how you think it will be
- Necessary growth and receptivity are the keys
- The right timing for your soul is not always in sync with your conscious mind
- Be patient
- Trust your abilities
- Be non-attached to outcome

Manifesting financial abundance
- Examine beliefs about money and worthiness
- Recognize your uniqueness, perfection and divinity
- It is God's desire for everyone to have abundance
- Living a deeply spiritual, God-centered life is not in conflict with financial success; you can have it all
- Look to the self, not past conditioning for the ability to receive
- Energy is energy. The universal energy of creation has no judgment
- Money, in and of itself, will not create happiness and fulfillment

Manifesting a romantic relationship
- Be romantic within the self
- Achieve the ability for vulnerability
- Become that which you seek in a partner

Doing vs. allowing
- Be aware of opportunities as they are presented
- Be discerning
- Get out of your own way
- Allow time to clear blockages necessary for manifestations

Instant manifestation
- Must have belief it can be so
- Collapses of time and space occur
- Very possible now in this new millennium
- Humanity is now beginning to remember that we have these abilities

Assistance from spirit guides and angels
- In the asking, assistance will be given
- They will not usurp your free will

Manifestation of your fears
- Be judicial in what you attach energy of thoughts to
- Universal energy will mirror that which you put out

Chapter 9

Health and Healing

"Health is an awareness of the physical structure and what it needs.
Healing is ultimately manifesting balance or wholeness through
integrating body, mind, and spirit."
—THEO

As we begin to recognize our self as the pure energy that we are, expanded consciousness and greater awareness of our physical structure follows. The remembrance of our self as a multidimensional being assists in understanding how the subtle energy bodies affect the healthful functioning of the physical body. Energy medicine, in all of its forms, is being accepted by the Western medical community as a reputable and helpful complement to allopathic treatment. We are waking up to the ancient knowledge of the indigenous cultures. We recommend that you integrate both forms of medicine into your wellness program.

The power of the mind to heal is widely acknowledged and is closely aligned with the impact of our emotions on our physical well-being. Unresolved emotional patternings, particularly those that manifest as anger or judgment of others, will form energetic blockages within the physical structure that can cause disease. Conversely, a compassionate or loving response carries with it a much higher and more healthful frequency, or vibration, thus impacting the body in a positive and healthful way. In his book *Walking Between the Worlds: The Science of Compassion,* author Gregg Braden does an excellent job of sharing the ancient teachings of the Essenes concerning compassion and other emotions, and how these as frequencies affect our overall well-being.

THEO reminds us that our purpose for choosing to be in a human form is to learn emotions. We encourage you to be aware of your emotions, not to repress or deny them. Give them their voice and acknowledge the need to integrate them on a soul level. Doing this will release the energy in your body and allow for a more healthful state.

Needless to say, proper nutrition, regular exercise, and daily meditation all contribute to your physical well-being. Don't wait to get sick before you start taking care of yourself. Attention to preventive or proactive treatments from traditional and holistic practitioners is highly recommended. Listen to your body and what it tells you it needs. Take the time to determine what your body is allergic to and what it needs more of.

We encourage you to look beyond the obvious and to begin to perceive yourself as an energy system that requires conscious management and fine-tuning in order to achieve and maintain its peak frequency. This peak frequency carries with it optimum physical health, blissful and deeply fulfilling emotional wellbeing, and expedition of your dreams and desires. It is that powerful! We ask you to love yourself enough to look at the people and situations in your life that deplete or nourish your energy. An honest assessment might lead you to some necessary and uplifting life changes. In her book *Why People Don't Heal and How They Can,* author and teacher Caroline Myss, Ph.D., does a masterful job explaining how the detachment of energy to old wounds, of being the victim, while gaining awareness of ourselves as finite human energy fields affects health and healing in our lives.

Are you stuck in the muck of blaming others for your life circumstances? Taking responsibility for your emotional and spiritual growth, welcoming change into your life, and fully embracing growth opportunities will lead you to greater health. It's time to get over the emotional wounds that might be holding you back.

There has been much research in recent years showing the power of prayer in nonlocal healing. If there is no time or space, and we are all connected energetically and accept the powerful premise that our thoughts and words are the creative force, it follows that focused, intentful prayer could affect the healing process. Dr. Larry Dossey presents remarkable evidence of this in his book *Reinventing Medicine.* In it he shares the results of numerous studies that overwhelmingly point to the reality of nonlocal healing. Again, it seems likely that we are only acknowledging that which has been known by many cultures for thousands of years. THEO cautions us that in the arena of praying for another's healing, it may not be in the highest good of that soul to be healed. With all nonlocal healing intentions, consider asking in prayer or meditation for permission on a soul level. Always send intentions that are for the highest good of the soul.

Our personal regimen for healthful living includes balancing holistic and cutting-edge modalities with traditional medical care, assistant to our daily routine which includes yogic breathing, meditation, and exercise.

We ask you to consider how important it is to love yourself enough to be able to love your neighbors. Get a massage. Meditate. Learn to say no. Watch the sunset. Find a waterfall and hang out for the day. Nourish your soul.

What is your definition of illness and disease?

Illness or disease in a physical structure is that which is being out of balance physically. The body is out of balance, then there is disease.

Can you define "out of balance" for us?

It is the functioning of the physical structure when it is imbalanced nutritionally, emotionally, and spiritually, then the body is functioning with blockages of energy within the physical structure that then create an imbalance or a malfunction.

What can we do to create and maintain a healthy balance of body, mind, and spirit?

It is the full soul integration that is necessary for the fulfillment on a spiritual level, as well as an emotional level, as beings come into contact with all aspects of their being, and patterns that no longer work, and issues and patterns set up in the physical structure. For it is emotions that do block energies in the physical body. It is also if one is fully aware of the nutritional balance and what the body speaks to you that it needs, meaning that if it is lacking in some nutrition, then there would be an imbalance there as well. If there is a genetic circumstance in which there is an imbalance in the genetics of the physical structure from birth, then that should be addressed as well. And one can use all forms of assistance to come into balance, whether it is nutrition, proper eating, supplementation of nutrients that cannot be absorbed from food that is eaten, chemistry balancing, such as hormonal intake if there is not enough hormones present in the physical structure. If there is a breakdown of a particular function of organs, then supplementation to assist, to back up if you would, to assist that organ function. So when one is fully aware of what the body needs, fully aware of the emotional balances necessary, then that leads to a balance in spirit, or soul integration. Fulfillment.

Could you explain the relationship between the flow of energy through our physical body and disease?

The process is that there is a blockage or a pooling of energy in a particular area of the body that is not functioning fully, meaning that energy has begun a block and then there is a backup in the system of its function, a breaking down of its function. One can utilize many modalities to assist that balancing, whether it be as the balancing of the electromagnetic field, the balancing of the polarities of the body, the balancing of the nutrition of the body, or the chemistry of the body, and, on the emotional level, coming into an awareness of all the patternings and how they began and how one can resolve issues of the past from within.

Can you speak more to the balancing of the energies in our body and how we can go about doing that?

There is a life pulse or flow of energy in the body that is the soul, or the spark of creation. There is also electricity, the electromagnetic field. When one balances the energy, there is a flow, or a pulse in the body of all the functioning that is happening whether it be the flow of the blood, or the organs, or the emotions. And that can be tested in the pulses of the body. If there is an erratic pulse in one area, one can then find that area in which there is blockage or imbalance, through energy balancing, or hands-on energy balancing and pulses. There are energy meridians, electric energy meridians within the body that can be utilized with acupressure, acupuncture, or Jin Shin Jitsu. Holding these points of energy within the body allows for an ignition. We would say it this way. Igniting a proper balance when there is an interruption, and then a restarting. Equal flows in the physical structure right and left.

How important is our thinking in regards to our personal health and in our ability to heal others?

Thinking is important, projection of thought. As in all life processes healing as well, the assistance of facilitating the healing of others, it is important that one has clarity within oneself as well. To integrate fully allows the being to be more fully functional in the assistance of others as well.

How does the healing process actually work when we assist others with the "laying on" of our hands?

. . . the utilization of another's ability to transmit electrical frequencies to balance; using one's electromagnetic field body as a conduit to draw universal energies through the body for balancing the energies of another. So a hands-on healer, as you put it, can be thought of as a conduit or a facilitator of that energy as it flows through. It is also a conduit and allows the energy of the physical being worked upon to flow through it and out as well. The key here to a healer of this type, it is necessary not to hold the energy of the other in your body. It is important to allow that energy to flow through and out.

How can we be most aware of making sure that happens?

There is an awareness of the energy of the other in the body where there is disease or blockage. One healer would feel it in the exact place in their body as it is in the client or the person in need—it is a confirmation. But to continue to hold the energy for the other person in that place within your own body, as the healer, is inappropriate. To know that that is only a confirming experience of knowing where to go and how to assist, and then let it be released from your physicality.

I have always been fascinated by how that transference of energy takes place, when we feel the exact blockage within our physical bodies as that of the person being worked on. How does that work?

Your bodies are very much the same in their working. As a facilitator, one absorbs the electromagnetic field of the other.

Through our intent?

It is an intent, but it is also the bodies responding in likeness, and an openness in receptivity, awareness.

Will the future of energy medicine be that it continues to grow dramatically in acceptance and popularity?

It would. For many would seek it out as a modality for wellness, not illness, for balance, maintenance; before there is such an imbalance that it creates disease or illness; to nip it in the bud, so to speak.

So we see people in increasing numbers integrating this into their wellness or wholeness programs?

Correct. In the honoring of self.

It also facilitates multidimensional experiences, doesn't it?

If that is the intent, yes.

Are we working in different dimensions when doing this work?

Yes, but there is a place of intent. If there is an intention of utilizing the energies for the healing, it does bring about multidimensional experiences in the sense of integration for those seeking the balancing. There is a witnessing because of the empathetic expression for the practitioner to experience the multidimensional experience of those worked upon, because of the empathetic connection.

What role does intuition and guidance front our angelic guides play in this type of healing?

Largely influenced. Intuitiveness is a sensitivity. Awareness. Empathy. Connectedness. In the asking for guidance, there can be guidance given by those mentors that are about who have expertise, to assist the facilitator. In the asking it is given.

In our personal process what type of meditation can we be Practicing daily to keep us most healthful?

The form that is psychologically and emotionally comfortable to you. Meditation is physiologically excellent, for it allows a rest for the nervous system; it allows a quietness; it allows the body to come into balance. So a meditation is a function that assists in the whole body balance.

Many healings have been reported to take place through the Power of prayer. Can you explain to us how this works?

Intent, focusing energy on a particular personality, brings about a focus energetically that assists the healing. There is that which is an awareness of the imbalance, where it is; in a focus upon that, allows for healing. The prayer to bring a personality into their wholeness, allows and facilitates their soul. It speaks to the soul in its creative abilities to heal itself. There are different forms of remote healing. Prayer healing is oftentimes that which is good intent placed upon the person who has illness or disease. To come to its highest or optimum health or good, it is important, however, that one engaging in this manner asks permission from the soul if it is appropriate that this be done.

In meditation?

Yes.

Simply by placing the question out there for permission?

Yes. But know that even if the prayer is given, the intention is always to help. There is good intent and can assist at that given time for betterment and ease, but when one witnesses that there is a prayer service or a group intent for healing, and there is a period of time of balance, and then the body reverts back to its imbalance, one can ascertain that that is not its soul's intent for its healing. When one places intent, one cannot know which is the highest good. When asking for permission, good thought, heartfelt thought, for wholeness and well-being is the best attitude, however that comes about.

There is more acceptance today for alternative healing modalities. Do you see in the near future the American Medical Association finally acknowledging these alternative techniques to be integrated with allopathic medicine?

Yes. For there are many that do incorporate the alternative, as it is said, or the natural, or wholeness of being into their medical practices; it is as a whole, or as a group. There does come about this out of the desire of humanity and its acceptance. For healers, medical professionals, all of these personalities are beings of service. If there is a service requested, would they not be wise to administer it if possible?

Are we going to see insurance companies accepting these alternative healing practitioners?
Yes. It has already begun.

So there is a full integration occurring between the alternative and the conventional healing communities.
Correct.

How do you see the future of the health care industry in the United States and throughout the world?

Improved. There will be continual discoveries within the medical communities, within the global community of medicine and sciences that bring about an understanding one unto the other. The sciences and the arts are very profound in bringing about a global community. You would find within the medical community, within the sciences, interaction throughout the world to bring about more healthfulness. You would be pleased.

Today we have millions of people unable to afford health insurance and are unable to receive quality health care. Do you see every citizen eventually being able to receive quality medical care?

Yes.

How does this come about?

Some would fight against it in the sense of feeling that some of their freedoms are usurped. But it comes about by all humanity engaging in agreement that it is necessary for the medical fields and professions in hospitals and places of bringing about balance to come into agreement in the assistance of humanity. They are servers to humanity. There would be a shift of consciousness about that. For in the past, in the old beliefs, there has been a relinquishing of power. It will be regained by the masses.

We have a lot of miraculous healing taking place on the planet today. Could you share with us how these miraculous healings occur?

Through the intent of the individual. The asking of the individual, that they be healed, and the openness and receptivity to that on a soul level. Then it can occur. Not always does the conscious mind know what the soul is asking. But ultimately if you were to speak to a personality that had a miraculous healing, you would be informed that they asked for assistance and they opened themselves for that.

There is a lot of interest and receptivity to shamanic healing methods that are known to be effective in the indigenous cultures. Is this interest likely to increase?

It would, but it would be more utilized because there will be a greater understanding of it. It has been cloaked in that which is the mysterious. What comes about in this time, in the millennium, is a greater understanding of the ability to administer and to facilitate the wholeness of being, the integration of soul, that allows for the wholeness of the physical structure and the proper functioning. So there will be greater awareness, not cloaked in that which is secretive.

How is it that the shaman uses the power of animals in his shamanic journey to heal the physical body?

They use it as a focus, to keep the consciousness focused so that the subconscious can then facilitate the healing. There are those who need to have a vision or a projection of the vision to keep the conscious mind busy as the subconscious works are done. A focus.

You are talking about for the practitioner here?

The practitioner. As to the individual, they receive the projection of thought from the healer. Because they then place the trust of that within the being facilitating, they accept it.

Because they believe they can heal?

Yes. There are aspects of the personality of the animal that have been attributed to the animal that speaks to them on a soul level about themselves. As there are animals, totem animals, from this belief system, each individual does have animals that they relate to in the sense of symbolism, that are of the earth, and the qualities of these animals are a part of the qualities of the human.

When we see these animals in our own meditations and journeys, are we getting confirmation regarding certain aspects of ourselves?

Yes. They are empowering as well.

Would you explain how a serious illness can be transforming on a soul level? Are these illnesses actually created as an opportunity for growth?

It is created for an opportunity of growth by the soul, it is an opportunity of awakening to abilities heretofore one was blocked to, or ignorant of. It allows beings to come more fully into their heart and out of their head to implement an integrative process on a soul level. A very powerful process, it allows one to be more aware and cognitive of the physical functioning and its relationships to the spirit and the mind. It is an awakening process for many.

With heightened consciousness in the new millennium, will people have to experience the terrible pain associated with so many illnesses?

Pain is a way of the body speaking to the imbalance therein. Whether it is blocked energy from an emotional situation that has not been allowed to flow through or that which is a blockage of thought or experience. As beings integrate on a soul level there will be less and less pain in the physical structure.

How can we cure addictions?

You live in an addictive world; the human body can become addictive; the human mind does become addictive. There are many forms of addictions. But when one comes fully into their soul in a fulfillment on a soul level, and an awareness of all the patternings, the emotional patternings, that are within, and through that understanding a release of old beliefs, there is a release of addictions as well. Addictions are only ways of filling up the void or incompleteness, or misunderstanding, or imbalance, in the being.

So it is indicative of a fragmented soul?

Yes.

In addition to what you shared with us about the soul integration process, what else can people do to rid themselves of their addictions?

Integrate into wholeness of being. Allow a voice to the little orphans. Allow the self the inner communication. Allow that which has been repressed to surface, to be seen and released.

Can you address the many claims that are being made throughout the world regarding cures that have been discovered for many of the terminal illnesses such as AIDS and cancer, but still appear to be unavailable to us?

For some they do cure; for others, they do not. We have been speaking about that all along. There would be more addressed in the sense of curatives, but one is not completely cured unless they do the inner work and trust the self. For the imbalance would continue to reoccur if there is not a balance in all areas of one's being.

What actually causes cancer and how does it form in the physical body?

All bodies are susceptible to cancer; it is a virus within the body that becomes activated, in cells that are predisposed to this activation. If there is an imbalance emotionally, an upset, it can be activated. If there is a continual emotional response to life, such as anger, it can create this in the structure, out of the stress placed upon the body when the energy is not free-flowing.

Can you speak to the enormous number of people on the planet that are now being infected with AIDS and the purpose of that on a soul level?

There are many that are not to be in the new millennium because of the intensity and the requirement on a soul level. They are not ready for it or they are to work from other dimensions rather than fully embodied and limited to that physical existence. So it is a form of disease that allows many to leave the physical into the spirit. But it is an awakening, to the world, that there is the necessity of a global community. For if there is health and healing in a global communication, then all beings have the availability to be in full health. As in the sharing of information and tools throughout the world, with humanity, wherever they may be, brings about a global sharing, one country unto another, one human unto another. Such as this will come about, so that there is a global human healthful state. It is about time.

Why does the soul choose to remain in physical form when the consciousness appears to have left, such as with people who have Alzheimer's?

There is a form of consciousness that is left or it would not. However, as this would continue, the body eventually would be relinquished.

When Alzheimer's patients die, do they then return to optimum consciousness as it related to what they take with them at that time?

The soul has their ultimate consciousness. Yes.

Will Down's syndrome and autistic children be able to physically and intellectually function more effectively in the new millennium?

Yes. There will be a shift and a change that will assist them chemically and functionally to bring about a better functioning brain. There would also be a better understanding in the sciences as to how this occurs within the environment of the physical. It is genetic oftentimes. And there will be more information as to genetics so that this would not occur.

Dolphins are thought to have extraordinary healing powers. We have spoken to many people who have had experiences that confirm that. Can you explain the energy associated with dolphins as well as with other animals?

There is a pureness of love that radiates out, unconditional love, in these circumstances of healing. For animals have not the cognition to delineate, or delete their energy from functioning, healing. There is a radiance. We are speaking specifically about the dolphin. The dolphin is a high-frequency animal, highly intelligent, nonaggressive, unconditionally loving, and that is what is radiant from them as beings encounter them. That then balances the energy of the individual to a higher frequency. When in contact with a perfectly balanced physical, one then can mimic it. They are energy balancers because of their high frequency, by their presence.

With the dawning of the new millennium and the soul integration process, what of the youthening that we see many physical bodies currently experiencing?

As beings incorporate these tools of fulfillment, of recognition of the soul, the physical body then has fewer blockages within it—in the emotional body as well as the physical— and there is a free-flowing energy that maintains the body at its optimum existence, not depleting it. So then in turn there does become a timelessness about the physicality, for there is nothing in its functioning to age it. It is the imbalance that is aging.

Any other thoughts on health and healing?

It is desired that all beings live in full health. It is desired that all beings live in fullness of self and wholeness. It can be achieved, and it will be achieved. Place the intent of wholeness within the self. It is a gift.

�֍ *Reflections on Health and Healing*

Definition of illness and disease
- Body out of balance
  - Nutritional imbalance
  - Emotional imbalance
  - Spiritual imbalance
  - Blockages of energy manifest as dis-ease

How to maintain healthy balance of body, mind, and spirit
- Become fully soul integrated. Awareness of patternings that no longer work. What are the core issues? Allows emotions to be experienced and released. This will help eliminate energy blockages within the body.
- Be aware of nutritional imbalances.
- Recognize genetic circumstances.
- Are you hormonally imbalanced?
- Listen to the body. Pay attention.

Relationship between flow of energy through the body and disease
- Energy will back up, creating a blockage when unresolved emotional issues are present.
- This blockage will create disease.
- Be aware of lifestyle and stress levels.

How to keep the physical body balanced energetically
- Supplementation
- Proper nutrition
- Energy meridian balancing
  - Acupressure
  - Acupuncture
  - Jin Shin Jitsu
  - Reiki

- Hands-on healing/chakra balancing
- Applied kinesiology/reflexology

The power of thought
- They are the creative force.
- Positive thought creates positive results.
- You must have clarity within yourself for complete physical wholeness.
- Be aware of projecting your imbalances to others or of you absorbing theirs. You must protect yourself and others energetically.

Hands-on healing
- Healers use their own electromagnetic field as a conduit for drawing in universal energies.
- He or she assists in the release of blocked energies within the body being worked upon.
- Be aware of letting the energy flow through and out of the body, fully releasing all energies that are absorbed.
- Place intention.
- Healer must know his or her own body.
- Be aware of emotions.

The future of energy medicine
- Energy medicine will be accepted by the medical community as necessary for total wellness.
- Proactive healing—not reactive—is excellent for regular maintenance.

Multidimensional aspects of spiritual or energetic healing
- Empathetic modality
- Engaging with another on a cellular level
- Assistance given from higher dimensions

- Must be open and receptive to available guidance
- Client/patient must have beliefs that it can be so

Meditation for optimum health
- Must choose a form that is physically and emotionally comfortable, excellent physiologically
- Allows a rest for the nervous system
- Greatly assists the body-mind-spirit balance

How does prayer affect healing?
- Energy is focused to assist healing.
- Recognizes the soul in its creative abilities to heal
- Asks permission from the soul
- The highest learning of the soul of the person being prayed for might be not to heal.

The future of health care throughout the world
- Improved, profound discoveries
- Blending of allopathic and alternative techniques
- Global communication and sharing
- People will demand and receive health insurance for all

Miraculous healings
- There must be an asking.
- Patient must have an openness and receptivity.
- Shamanic healing methods will become more accepted, less mysterious.
- Fully integrated souls have these miraculous healing abilities.

Transformational powers of illness and disease
- Dramatic growth opportunities, greater awareness
- Becoming more cognizant of the physical functioning
- Allows you to recognize your abilities

- Stimulates thinking from the heart first, then the head
- Creates opportunity for spiritual awakening

Addictions
- Living in an addictive world
- Easy for body and mind to become addicted
- Indicative of a fragmented soul
- Soul integration replacing addictive behavior with love and self-esteem
- Allowing all that has been repressed to surface

Chapter 10

Death and Dying

"The soul chooses to leave the physical body at the perfect time."
—THEO

What is it about death and dying that brings fear to our hearts? Is it the termination of our consciousness, of our very self? Do we fear that we haven't lived our lives righteously and soon will be judged accordingly . . . that we might end up in a place called hell? Or is it the fear and dread of the physical pain many accept as an inevitable part of the dying process? Whatever the source of this trepidation we believe that there is no reason to fear death or the process of dying. THEO's teachings about the soul's process of transitioning from this lifetime into the next confirm that which has been reported by millions of people who have had near-death experiences. The past thirty years have produced abundant research confirming that our consciousness does survive physical death and that the process of "crossing over" may be the grandest spiritual experience of them all.

In her groundbreaking book *On Death and Dying,* our good friend Dr. Elisabeth Kübler-Ross identifies the five stages of dealing with death: denial and isolation, anger, bargaining, depression, and acceptance. We recommend anything written by Elisabeth on the topics of death, dying, and the afterlife, and that you remember these five stages when dealing with the process in your own life experiences.

Those who have participated in the hospice movement know of the spiritual, even mystical, experiences inherent in this kind of work. Our personal experiences with the dying have left us feeling blessed and honored to have been a part of someone's last days. The process often is more difficult for the living than it is for the dying.

It has been said that if we have no fear of dying, then we will have no fear of living. We encourage resolution and forgiveness in all relationships prior to making the transition.

What is the emotional, physical, and spiritual process of the soul leaving the physical body at the time of death?

The soul becomes fully aware that it is time to depart the physical structure, for it is a choice of the soul to end that incarnation. There is a release, as it were, as the soul leaves the body, particularly through the crown of the head, much in similarity to that which is out-of-body experiences. Some can leave through the heart area or the head. There is a floating above the body which is a realization that the body has released the soul, or the soul has released the body. There are mentors, teachers, and angelic beings, as well as members of family close to one, to support the adjustment that is in the other dimension. There is a bit, at times, for some, a disorientation to what has happened. There are these assistants, let us say, to make an ease in transition. When this has occurred, there is not the electricity, as it could be determined to maintain the creative activity in the physical structure that continues the functioning of the body and the cognitive abilities of the mind. The body can continue to function, however, with external stimulus provided it. That is not soul motivated. When the soul leaves the body, and the body is not stimulated externally, it will diminish its activity and stop. Then, as with all living things, there is a deterioration process of form.

When you speak of the cognition of the mind at the time of death, are you speaking of the brain?

The brain functioning, yes. The cognitive part of the brain will not function any longer.

What about our consciousness, then?

That is part of the consciousness. Cognitation is conscious awareness and abilities. The functioning of the physical body through the brain can continue for a period of time that which can activate the musculature.

Do we take with us at the time of release our conscious awareness and memories of this lifetime?

Yes.

So we have awareness of the fact that we are leaving our bodies at the time of death?

Yes. That is soul awareness, you see. The soul is the aware aspect of the body.

Speak more to that, please.

The soul is that which would be the ability to understand, the ability to create, the ability to remember, that is soul functioning.

What impact do our spiritual beliefs have upon the actual process of dying?

One's belief does affect one's experience. For the thought is the creative process—is it not?—and the receiving process. To receive information, one receives and perceives from those beliefs, and reacts.

If we believe in eternal life, will we have a different experience than if we do not?

If there is a belief that the soul is ongoing, does not die, and that then it is going somewhere else, other than a physical structure, or to another physical structure, whatever the belief may be, there is a realization in a much more rapid way of the experience of transition, completion, release, birth, into a new experience. If the belief is that of darkness, then there is much more time of an adjustment to what is, and the need for guidance.

So we do create or affect the transition process based on our beliefs at the time of death?

Yes. Now, in particular circumstances, there can be a personality that has not a belief of anything after the physical experience in the conscious mind. However, on a soul level, one must be evolved enough to have that belief. It has not translated into the consciousness that their experience of choosing life, choosing a bodily experience, an environment that supports a nonbelief out of learning process, whatever that may be, upon leaving the body will then still have, on a soul level, a realization of an ongoing energy. Know that we are speaking in generalities, and the general rule of one who is a younger soul, let us say, that has no soul belief and understanding of a relinquishing of a physical body at the time of death and an ongoing energy would have an adjustment with teachers on the other side to that understanding. However, if there is a personality, a soul that is engaged in the physical structure in a particular environment of nonbelief, conscious nonbelief, yet the soul in its depth knows, but the external or the human being, the consciousness of the human being, would not adhere to that because of environment upon their passing from that dimension, the physical dimension, into what is called afterlife, heaven, or whatever you perceive it to be, another dimension, birthing into a new dimensional experience, it would be different. If the soul is evolved enough to have that recognition, it would not be as dark of a transition or the need of the support of spiritual teachers, guides, angelic beings, whatever, as the other. So it is individual. We cannot give you a statement completely encompassing all.

How important is having resolution with all aspects of our lives at the time leading up to death?

We have been speaking to it. It is full soul integration.

So it is the feeling of peace and resolution prior to the transition?

Yes. And acceptance.

Can you explain the concept of surrender, particularly as it relates to not fighting death?

It is coming into acceptance, is it not? And then an allowance. When one has come into this surrender or the allowance of the inevitable, one can live the life more fully, can they not? For one would not block experience and be fully present moment to moment.

When we have an out-of-body experience, does this give us a pretty clear glimpse of what the experience will be when we actually make the transition?

It gives one experience, yes. Not all have clarity.

Is conscious dying to include the ability to simply decide to leave the body one last time when the physical form no longer works? To leave the body by choice without committing suicide?

Each death, as it were, is a suicide, is a choice, for suicide is a choice. That is alarming to many when we use this word, for it is very much a fearful word. But ultimately what a suicide is a choice of death. Most often when people choose suicide, they choose by their own hand or their own doing to extinguish life. Ultimately, when one dies, the soul chooses to relinquish the body. So in essence, there is great similarity, is there not? Only one way is more conscious than others, for some. But not always are they from a balanced point of view. The suicides are most often from an imbalance. It is not so much that, as the completion with the life challenges or learnings that were to be had. So there is a choosing of relinquishment of the physical that no longer serves it. So it is not necessarily the relinquishment of the body because they know it is happier or better.

It is just time.

It is time, and to note herein, that it is only different. There is great love, there is great peace, but there are also opportunities in other dimensional experiences for challenges and growth. So to give up one arena of growth for another ... they are only different, are they not?

So the answer to the question is that we can do this when we have cocreated this decision on a soul level, when the physical body is no longer working?

Or in need.

How can we eliminate both the fear of death and the attachment to the physical experience?

Beings, individuals, can eliminate fear by accessing their soul and incorporating all aspects of being. In that fulfillment of soul and the sense of peacefulness and happiness within its being, there is greater ease in relinquishing the physical structure at the appropriate time, for then there would be a soul knowing that there is completion. To do that eliminates fear, as well, does it not? The answer is twofold there, for there are two answers, two questions answered in one statement.

Do we know before we enter this incarnation how long we are going to live?

Yes.

And what kind of physical death we might experience?

No. That is cocreated.

What of the relationship between the soul's plan, or divine blueprint, and our free will?

The soul directs the free will of man, ultimately. The soul is an integral part of the human being. It is not separate from. It chooses to incarnate. It chooses its path. It cocreates the circumstances in which it learns soul lessons and soul opportunities and soul challenges, how they are met. One is not separate from the other.

We feel a tremendous amount of pain from the deaths of our children or loved ones who die in tragic, horrible ways. It is difficult to rationalize or understand why this would happen.

Why would God do that?

Yes.

That is placing responsibility outside the individual. It is difficult to understand why a soul would choose a particular circumstance that at one point would seem horrific or violent. But it is to understand as well that their body is a tool, it is a vehicle, and that in the experiences that are attracted to this soul are opportunities of learning for that soul, but not only limited to the individual soul. Know that all beings that are connected, interconnected with that particular personality, learn from the experience as well. The learning is never only for one, you see, and it may be for greater numbers than one, in that sense that it affects the world.

Does a soul enter a fetus that will eventually be aborted?

Know that the soul enters into a physical structure when it fully realizes that that physical structure will be fully functioning on earth. There is not a point of a soul entering into a fetus unless it will come to fruition. Souls are very aware. There would be no point in that for the learning for the soul. However, that circumstance for the parents or the birthing mother, and those choices therein made, the soul of that personality has chosen those experiences for their learning. So one cannot judge another's experience. Again, it is repetitive. For each soul chooses perfectly along its path what is appropriate for its growth. And that is to be trusted. It is arrogant for another to determine those choices for an individual.

So, would the answer to that question be the same as it relates to miscarriages and stillbirths?

Yes. But know because many of these mothers have experienced the soul, have had contact with the soul that is about to enter into a physical structure, so there is angst on the mother's part that they have done something wrong, or something has been missed, or that that soul has missed an opportunity. Not so.

Speak more to that, please.

In the sense of a stillbirth or a miscarriage, that it could be possible the soul not coming to fruition in a physical structure had missed an opportunity. There are no missed opportunities. The soul desiring to incarnate will have that opportunity. Desiring to incarnate with the particular parent for the parenting process or the interaction of family will have that opportunity.

How do you perceive the current state of hospice care on our planet?

It has been very good. It is acknowledged the care of the terminally ill and the need of those personalities to share and to be nurtured and cared for.

What is most important for us to remember as we provide hospice care?

Communication; it is extremely important. Not ignoring the fact that this person is dying, speak about it, be fully communicative about it, not uncomfortable in its discussion, allowing the individual to speak about their feelings. Communication is the most important. There would be opportunities to give medications, to do the physical caregiving, as to comfortableness. But the care of the emotions is extremely important.

And listening.

Yes.

How do you see hospice care evolving now into the new millennium?

It evolves into taking into account spirit. That which would be the soul, the integrative process, encouraging that.

Is the guidance provided by beings such as yourselves a part of hospice care in the future?

When requested. There are individuals who are involved in consciousness and aware that they can have contact with guidance and teachers and mentors such as we. And, in the asking, it can be given unto them. But it must be by request.

Is the soul aware of what is being done or said when in a coma, and how can we learn to communicate with the patient when in this state?

Yes, there is an awareness. The soul is aware. As to the caregivers' perceptions? It is a matter of trust in the ability to continue to communicate to them, drawing them into this dimensional experience, maintaining connectedness. For it is in that period of time for many a time of choosing.

Would they be having at that time experiences that would be similar to a near-death experience?

Yes. Not all remembered, however.

But they are in and out of their body quite a bit at that time?

Correct.

And how can we best communicate with people when in these states?

As you can with all people: intent, quieting the mind, focusing the mind, and proceed. Trust in it, do not negate it with a negative thought that it cannot be done. For if one negates it with a thought that it cannot be so, it cuts the connection, as if you were speaking on the telephone and you would hang up the receiver.

How do you see the future for euthanasia and assisted suicide?

Is that not a choice? Agreements made among peoples not to take extraordinary circumstances to maintain life. As in euthanasia, that which would be the choice of the individual, would it not? As well as assisted suicide, very similar.

Some legal challenges as far as that goes, however.

Yes, but when one honors another being, not judging them, then there can be dialogue about it that is not as highly charged emotionally by those beings who are fearful.

I would like you to speak to the activities of the last several years of Jack Kevorkian.

One must be aware of one's intention.

Has he helped or hurt the conscious-dying movement?

He has brought it to the forefront, which was necessary for dialogue, discussion, and awareness. As to his activity, it was self-motivated ultimately, surrounding his feelings of inadequacy and his own issues in his life.

What are your views regarding capital punishment?

It is important for all beings to take responsibility for their actions. To follow the rules that are set by society is important and in that there needs to be repercussion for activities that have not followed the rules. As it has been stated, "An eye for an eye, and a tooth for a tooth," yes? More importantly described, it is a responsibility of all individuals to respect life, yes, to respect another's life. But it is important to have structure, for there are personalities that act out in society and should be taken into account. As to the right or wrong, it is not our judgment. As to the necessity of boundaries, yes, whatever form that may be.

A soul enters into an incarnation and shoots thirteen kids in Littleton, Colorado, then leaves the planet at its own hand. What soul growth comes from that type of experience?

There is the necessity of looking at those actions as a whole, on a soul level. But it is also taken into account the choosing of each soul to participate in a teaching for the planet, an awakening for the planet.

That which is happening in the outer experiences of your earth, your interactions, is but a reflection of the upheaval from within the individuals. So it is a requirement of society, as it were, to be more aware. It is not a judgment one unto the other, but to look at the circumstance that is present upon the planet, gain from it, integrate from it within the individual self and express love externally, fully of the self, and then one can express love of others. This was not so in these individuals.

Is there positive and negative soul growth?

It must be assessed in its passing to what was gained, what was experienced, what is needed for reflection.

The question had to do with individual soul growth.

The soul growth does come about from the actions and reactions and the need to integrate it, however that may come about.

So what was the purpose of the soul that shot those teenagers?

That is all individualistic.

Can you give us some last words regarding death and dying?

Death is a relinquishing of the body, the death of the physical structure. It is not the end of the soul's experience. Death is a birth as well. Dying is the process. Fear not either, for if one is soul integrated, one will have a full awareness of its process and be comfortable within it.

✤ Reflections on Death and Dying

The death and dying process

- The soul chooses to leave the body at the perfect time.
- There are mentors, teachers, and angelic beings present to assist in the transition.
- The soul can exit and return several times before its final exit.
- Your consciousness survives physical death as your soul possesses your cognitive abilities and awareness.
- The brain will not function once the soul has left the body for the final time.

How spiritual beliefs affect the transition process

- They affect the initial stages because our thinking is a creative force.
- Adjustments will be made, assistance given.
- Ultimately, the soul knows that it is eternal and this is made obvious to the consciousness at the time of transition.
- Each transition will be slightly different initially based upon the beliefs of the dying.

Importance of resolution prior to dying

- Full soul integration
- Forgiveness
- Allowance for the process follows acceptance of self.

Conscious dying

- Develop the ability to leave the body at will.
- Know that every death is the choice of the soul.
- Every death, ultimately, is a suicide.

Eliminating the fear of dying
- Full soul integration
- Experience yourself as more than your physical body.

Relationship between the soul's plan and free will
- The soul directs the free will of man.
- One is not separate from the other.
- Cocreate circumstances between free will and divine blueprint.

Why there are so many tragic deaths
- Many souls have incarnated as martyrs.
- The soul chooses its path perfectly.
- There are always profound growth opportunities for all involved.

Abortions, miscarriages, and stillbirths
- The soul only enters a human form that will be birthed.
- The soul is very aware. There would be no point in entering a fetus that would not come to fruition.
- It is inappropriate and arrogant to judge another's experience.
- There is much learning for all involved.
- There are no missed opportunities.

Hospice care
- Communicate; honor the requests of the dying.
- Be a good listener.
- Humanity is now more accepting of the integration of spirit, taking into account the soul.
- Angelic guidance is available in the asking.

Coma patients
- The soul is aware.
- They are frequently in and out of the body.
- Patients can be communicated with telepathically and verbally.

The future of euthanasia and assisted suicide
- It is a choice.
- It is inappropriate to judge another's intentions.
- Change and acceptance will come with communication and elimination of fear.

Chapter 11

Afterlife and Reincarnation

"There is no death; it is only the relinquishing of one form for another. As energy is constant, only the form changes."
—THEO

Insights into afterlife and reincarnation are limited to the experiences we manifest in our lives from within. The reported number of near-death experiences, out-of-body experiences, spontaneous past life recalls, and other dimensional shifts and collapses of time and space seem to have increased in recent years as humanity has awakened to other realities. Most people we talk to about this report having had some profound experience of feeling as though they have lived before, or have known something, for instance, that required some training that was never learned in this lifetime. Many people report having experiences in the lucid dreaming state that they can only interpret as being connected to a previous lifetime.

And why is it that for some people life seems so easy and fun, that they just appear so comfortable in their skin while always just seeming to get "it"? Those who are healers and teachers on our planet. And for others, life is just the opposite—experiencing disharmony in most areas of their lives, while creating karmic learning opportunities with many of their actions.

As we mentioned in previous chapters, THEO answers these questions in the concept of soul age. The difference between old souls and young souls is the amount of earth experience had by each soul, the learning of emotions experienced in previous lifetimes, the growth of the soul. For if we look around us, we can see a dramatic variance in the expressions of consciousness by various members of the human race. And it does not make one greater than another, just more experienced as a human being.

In the accounting of his life, *Autobiography of a Yogi,* Paramhansa Yogananda writes in great detail about his personal experiences with reincarnation while growing up in India. Dr. Brian Weiss, former chairman of the psychiatry department at Mount Sinai Medical Center in Miami, writes convincingly in his bestselling book, *Many Lives, Many Masters,* about his experiences with patients having profound past-life regressions while under hypnosis. The list of books detailing personal confirmations and experiences of past lives is extensive.

There is a well-documented story of a small child in India who led police to a man who had been her husband and who had murdered her a few years earlier in her most recent past lifetime. There is also an amazing story of two-year-old twin girls who began speaking a language that their parents couldn't understand. After extensive research, an ancient language expert finally concluded that it was an Aramaic dialect spoken at the time of Christ that hadn't been spoken in more than eighteen hundred years.

One of our favorite personal experiences occurred among the Havasupai on the Indian reservation at the bottom of the Grand Canyon. While participating in a Native American Sweat Lodge ceremony, we concurrently experienced a spontaneous past-life recall involving a seven-year-old Native girl with whom we had deeply connected. We experienced some sort of dimensional shift, or collapse of time and space, and as we recounted it to each other in detail, we realized that we had both just had the exact same experience. It was very confirming for us, as we had known since meeting each other that we had been together before.

THEO teaches us that when we leave this lifetime there are billions of choices of experience for the soul to choose from, including reincarnating in physical form and that it is ultimately the soul's choice. Heaven and hell are not places that we go to when we die but are states of being that we create for ourselves in and out of the physical body. The Kingdom of Heaven resides within us as our soul—there is no separation from God.

What is the afterlife really like? We probably won't know for sure until we get there, but our personal experiences beyond or out of our bodies suggest that we have nothing to fear. In fact, it will be more blissful and ecstatic than we can imagine. We have had many personal confirmations through THEO of communication with our deceased friends and relatives. One of our close friends, who recently died of cancer, told us after he died, "The light body is awesome," when asked what it is really like on the other side. We have witnessed hundreds of confirmations in our public experiences with THEO of people making contact and getting personal messages. We have no doubt that we survive physical death.

I would like to begin our discussion on the afterlife and reincarnation by revisiting the subject of God. What is the true essence or nature of God?

God is not one being sitting on a throne as many might perceive in their conscious mind of humanity. God is the creation or the spark of creativity of the entire universe. It is that which is the ultimate love that permeates all things, all beings: total unconditional loving energy that is present. That is how it can be best described.

Male and female energy equally?

Yes.

At the time of physical death, do we have an experience with this energy?

The peace and love that permeates the energetic dimensions will be *felt*. Yes.

How did God come to be?

It is a universal, or what many think of as a "big bang," or that full experience of the beginning of energetics. One has not a conscious picture of what could be.

Along those lines, then, how did our soul come to be?

The soul is an energetic that is a part of that "bang," or division of energies of the Creator.

Many people have shared with us their near-death experience. What is the truth of the experience of the afterlife?

As to the experience of the human as it leaves the body on a soul level and the sense of what one perceives as death, there is that which is the light that is extremely bright, and there is sound at times, many would hear sound, or music. There is that which would be the meeting of deities, or those personalities perceived as such in the beliefs of the individuals such as Jesus, at times, angelic beings, or other deities that are of other religious beliefs that are comforters to those personalities. There is that which is familiarity with those other souls who have passed that are recognized, to be in assistance to the transitional period, or process. There are teachers and mentors that lead the way and inform the soul of its transition if there is confusion. As to others' experiences, some experience a tunnel, moving quickly into the bright light. Others experience only the brightness. There are these experiences that are similar over again and again that are described by many.

What is the life review that people speak of?

That is part of the adjustment as they make the choices to stay within that dimensional realm, or heaven, as one might call it, or that which would be the returning again into the body. You are speaking of those transitional periods out-of-the-body when there are the decisions being made.

And then when we leave for the last time, do we then have a life review from the entire previous incarnation?

Yes, there is a knowing and understanding of the experiences of the most recent learnings, but one has access and understanding of all learning, and of the soul, fully.

Is there really, then, such a thing as heaven or hell?

There are perceptions of those places that can be created in the thought form. But in that experience or expression, it's not a reality fully, but that which would be a perception. And upon learning of this, then, one becomes more fully aware of their options.

Speak more to that, please.

Meaning that a soul has options or opportunities or other dimensions in which to interact. So as one becomes fully aware of the circumstances and the opportunity to choose, then that which would have been a perception from one embodiment as to heaven or hell, one has created. Then there is a realization that one can choose other experiences, and that this is but a perception or belief that is being carried over.

Is there any scientific proof of the reality of reincarnation?

There has been documentation of differing parts of the world wherein a child would be incarnate and in full memory of the most recent incarnation, and in doing such leads others to take note and to validate what they know.

Quite a few of these stories, actually.

Many of them, and there has been documentation of a crime or a murder being solved by a child who remembered being murdered in the most previous life, and it was proven. So that it is not so much scientific, but it is a confirmation, is it not?

Yes, and we read of many of those confirmations. Why is it so difficult for people to accept reincarnation as truth?

Oftentimes it is a fear base, it is a belief that it has been passed along in the family structure or the religious affiliations, and many fear to go against that which is being taught in their religion. But in many parts of the world, most believe in the ongoing soul essence.

Does the linear time of our death affect the immediate journey of the soul, from an astrological standpoint?

The soul is unencumbered once it has left the physical structure of the energetics of the earthly experience or the planets therein that influence it. For they are no longer attached to a physical that is affected.

There are still many souls that remain attached to the physical in the form of what we would perceive as ghosts or poltergeists. How do they finally move on and what is the purpose of staying attached to the earth plane when there is guidance available?

There is assistance but there are some souls who prefer to remain attached to the astral plane, or the physical existence of the earth, whether it be because of a certain circumstance, or other people, or a place. They remain attached, and when satisfied, whatever need it may be for that that attachment, will release to other dimensional realms. There are those who are killed at times in great numbers that have great confusion, such as a massacre, that remain attached for time because there is so much to attend to. Think in terms of mass hysteria. So there are those times when there is an attachment because there has not been an understanding and a release, and they are caught between the astral and other dimensions.

Do they then act as guides and provide assistance?

No. Those are what you call ghosts that interact.

What is the power that we possess in dealing with these entities?

Call upon the light and guidance and angelic beings to assist them, to open a portal for the light for them to go to. That is an assistance.

Release them in the sense of emotional connection as well, if it is one that one is emotionally tied to. Bless them on their way.

What happens during an exorcism, when there is a possession that has taken place?

This has been documented as well, and that is when a being wishes to continue an embodiment within the earthly experience attaches to a human. Oftentimes, there is susceptibility by that human in an attachment to them as well. It is also that there are as you would call poltergeists, which is more importantly to be recognized as energy that is erratic. It is not as much that which would be an entity.

Speak more to that, please.

Meaning that there are entities that are attached to the earthly plane that can do deeds of moving about physical objects. In that which is called poltergeist, which is erratic behavior of energy, is not always that which would be a soul that is attached to the earth. It is energy that is reflected by an adolescent, that is shifting energy in their body and has not consolidated it yet. Adolescents have very high energy and are very open and receptive to energetics, and there can be, in certain circumstances that are attractive to energetics such as this, the ability, or the energy being so erratic within an environment, that there is this kinetic energy that moves about. The power of thought is great and all beings have the ability to move energy. In an adolescent that is erratic and has this power, oftentimes it comes from them.

So in the case of an exorcism, what happens to the soul of the body that is being possessed by another entity?

There has been documentation of this, but most often it is a fragmented part of that soul that is confused, that is angry, that it is acting out.

So then the process is less one of exorcism than it is of soul integration?

Yes. But in this process what would be found in the time to come, there would be an emotional and psychological adjustment, meaning that it would be utilized not only by that which would be spiritual attributes, but that which would be psychological counseling— spiritual, physical, and psychological.

It is difficult for many people to accept that someone like Adolf Hitler is not burning in hell. What happens to the soul of such a monstrous human being?

Know there was a mental illness with this personality; however, charisma led many into that illness. However, again it is a nonjudgment, for there are many lessons within the earthly plane in the sense of the expression of those dualities. As to the specific personality, one would be responsible for their actions, but he was not alone. This was one personality that created horrific acts upon the earth, yes. There were those who were in belief of what he believed, that engaged with him that were as horrific, were they not, in their actions? There is the necessity of being responsible for those actions, in body or out of body. Accountability.

How does that accountability work in other dimensions?

There are guides, mentors, and angelic realms and dimensions in which they must work for that alignment, in what one might call forgiveness of self.

How does karma play into this, and what of future incarnations for a soul like that?

There would not be the gift of incarnating for some great time, would work in other dimensions first before that would be available.

So I am hearing then that there is a spiritual hierarchy of some kind that would guide this type of process and decision making?

Correct. But it is also to take note that it is not only this one. There have been many throughout your historical experiences of the earth. This one has the most fame.

And we have some on our planet today as well.

Yes, acting out the duality, the negative energy, out of their need for control, for power.

What of animals? Do they ever reincarnate as human beings?

No. However, animals do incarnate time and again. They do have souls. They are fully attached to the earthly experience. Humans incarnate as humans in that sense of a higher vibrational frequency in the cognitive abilities, that evolution.

As we evolve to higher levels of consciousness, will we be able to access past-life memories at will?

Yes. And that is what is coming about in the new millennium. There is a full awareness of experiences of the past that influence the present. That is soul integration.

How is it that soul families form and then make the decision to incarnate together?

It is a choice that they come together in physical. They are souls of the same age, same experience, same beliefs, same understanding, choosing that which would be supportive of one another's growth. The soul family is the same soul age, same vibrational frequency, energetically. Soul family is eternal. Not always are those who are blood-related soul family. At times it is such but not always.

How do we know and recognize that in one another?

There is a recognition of a soul family member, for there is an unconditional loving experience. One does not judge another even when one is not in agreement. For you are individuals with the experiences of self to incorporate, but there is an acceptance and respect that is understood and recognized and felt fully, physically as well as mentally and emotionally and psychically.

When we move into other dimensions following this lifetime can we take on human form in these other dimensions?

There are forms in other dimensions, in other planetary experiences, yes.

Are there other physical beings that are more spiritually evolved than us?

Not always. Different experiences.

Are there more spiritually evolved societies?

As one would perceive the hierarchy or the higher realms of spirit, the angelic beings, yes.

Do we have the opportunity to remain in physical form for a period of time in these other dimensional experiences following our death?

Yes. For there is that vibrational frequency, you see. The electromagnetic field.

Which creates for us that same sensation?

Correct. And that is true and has been documented and experienced with those who have had amputations. The sense and awareness of that which has been removed remaining.

Please speak to the concept of "no time."

That is a difficult concept to take into a linear mind, for the linear mind is familiar with the linear time concept. So it is most difficult to perceive in a conscious way of that timelessness, with the exception when one has had the experience of collapsing time. Meaning that being in a circumstance where time has elapsed and there has not been a knowing of it, or that there has been a bilocation that has happened. And there have been many that have experienced that, where they have been one place and in a short time, shorter than would be allowed in a normal linear experience, they are in another place. So there are experiences that humanity has had in the timelessness. Many, in terms of relationships, have a sense or a feeling of that timelessness in a relationship when they have a friend that they have not seen in years and pick up with them energetically as if there has been no space and time for their relationship to resume. So there are sensitivities, experiences, awareness of that expression of that truth, but it is experiential. We cannot describe unto you what it is.

It appears that we are now living in a time of more frequent collapses of time and space. Can you explain what takes place when this phenomena occurs?

Being fully present in the moment. That is where the awareness is focused and the collapse occurs. Children are very good at it. To be so totally focused that one then is oblivious to the linear movement of time. That is a life fully lived, for that is full experience.

Do you have any other thoughts regarding the afterlife and reincarnation?

As one moves forward into the experience and the memories herein in this full body awareness of the soul, there will be confidence in the ongoing experience of the soul that the body that is no longer useful gives way to new experiences. It is as if one puts on a suit of clothes and then the following day removes those clothes and puts on another. That is what a body is. The energy is constant, it is only form that is changed. That is the continuum. However, as the experience of awareness grows, and when one puts on that suit, or body, there will be full memory of the other body or suit that has been. In doing such, there is recollection of the lessons therein learned, which, in turn, brings about a better peacefulness within the experience, for there is a full resonance within the self, of self, soul self, centered in the soul. Centered in the self. Not self-centered, as in the sense of egotism, but in the truth of one's being. Blessed is that.

✤ *Reflections on Afterlife and Reincarnation*

Revisiting the question "What is the true essence or nature of God?"
- Not one being sitting on a throne
- Creation or the spark of creativity of the entire universe
- Ultimate love that permeates all things, all beings
- Total unconditional loving energy
- Equal masculine and feminine energy
- The soul, an energetic that is part of the division of energies of the creator

The truth of the experience of transitioning to the afterlife
- A bright light and a tunnel for some, but not all
- Sound and music frequencies present
- Meeting with spiritual deities, family members, and angelic beings for comfort
- Teachers and mentors to lead the way if there is confusion

The life review
- Part of the adjustment to other dimensions
- Knowing and understanding of experiences in most recent reincarnation
- The soul, which retains memories

Is there a heaven or hell?
- Not a reality fully, only a perception
- Can be created in thought form, in our own experience
- Creating reality with our thinking
- The soul, which chooses its experiences

Is there proof of reincarnation?
- Many confirmations and documented stories

- children remembering most recent incarnation such as helping police solve their murder from most recent lifetime

Why people doubt reincarnation
- Fear
- Beliefs taught by family
- Religious restrictions, control issues

Souls that remain attached to earth for a time after physical death
- Remain attached to the earth plane or astral plane due to circumstance, person, or place
- Will release to higher dimensions when their attachment is satisfied
- Confusion or mass hysteria caused by massacres or large group killings
- Known as "ghosts"
- Assistance given by praying or meditating and requesting that they seek the light of higher dimensions
- Those who ask for angels to assist them to light portal

Exorcism
- Attachment of one soul to another that is still in human form
- Can also be a significant fragmented aspect of the being
- Spiritual and emotional imbalance
- Poltergeists, usually erratic energy not entities, that attach to adolescent children

What happens to souls like Adolf Hitler?
- Many lessons are in the sense of the expressions of earthly dualities.
- Soul would have to take responsibility for its actions during that lifetime. Cause and effect. Karma.

- Accountability would extend into other dimensional experiences.
- Much work would have to be done for a great period of time before the gift of incarnation would be available.
- A spiritual hierarchy does exist to guide the process and decision making.

Soul remembrance and soul families
- New millennium energetics create opportunities for higher vibrational frequencies to activate memories.
- Soul family members recognize one another.
- Same soul "age" and frequencies
- Incarnate together to support each other's growth

Concept of "no time"
- Impossible for linear mind to fully comprehend
- Full presence in the moment-to-moment experience
- Childlike perspective or behavior
- The lapse of linear time without conscious knowledge or remembrance
- Bilocation, being in two places at once
- Highly experiential

Chapter 12

The Future

"Through awakened consciousness, humanity fully experiences a thousand years of peace beginning in the year 2012."
—THEO

Congratulations on making it to the twenty-first century! It was touch and go there for a while but we made it, and now we get to see what this new future is really going to look like. THEO was very clear and accurate in stating that there would be virtually no repercussions from the rollover to the twenty-first century. Anticipating no problems, we observed the fear that this time instilled in many people. How fitting it now seems that the dawning of an age that has been prophesied to bring about the shift in humanity from fear to love, would, in fact, find all of our greatest fears at its inception.

As you have already heard in this dialogue, we believe that we are, indeed, standing in the doorway to the Age of Miracles. The only question that remains for each one of us is whether we walk through that doorway or not—it is a choice. For many, the next several years will not seem like a time of miracles at all. They will choose to ignore the opportunities present for inner growth, and will continue to attach all their power to the external world, ignoring the only place where miracles can be created, in the inner world of soul. And they won't manifest miracles in their lives because they don't believe they can. It's that simple!

How your external world unfolds in the years to come will be a reflection of your inner being, your inner process, an expression of the peace and fulfillment that you realize internally, how you really feel about yourself in the quiet moments. Our common external world too, will be a reflection of the internal process that leads to the collective consciousness achieved by humanity. We believe that the power of our thinking can lead to a silent revolution that suddenly won't be silent anymore. We will move mountains and make a difference in ways that we have not begun to imagine, and express our love for our planet and our brothers and sisters while writing new history.

The scientists and artists will bring about a global community. THEO has stated that the year 2012 will be the beginning of a thousand years of peace, and that the evolution of humanity will not reverse itself. It is our sense that the human experience is, indeed, growing to be very special and sacred—a remarkable school for soul growth.

As the primary subject of this book is full soul integration, we have limited this chapter to just a few questions on topics that could easily evolve into entire books. That THEO does not provide great detail here is partially due to the fact that the future is now being created and that you impact it tremendously with your every thought and deed. Angels or other nonphysical energies cannot usurp the free will of human beings, which places the responsibility (the ability to respond) for our future firmly on our shoulders. Thinking and acting impeccably while taking right action in our lives is the seed that grows into our desired future.

What is your perspective on the real meaning of the year 2000?

As beings move into the 2000 century numbers, it is that which is the age of spirit and exploration of the being, and the fulfillment of the human experience, meaning, that there is a recognition of one's full soul integration and a recognition of one's full self, that there is an energy about the earth presently that allows for beings to be fully integrated and allows for beings to be fully aware—consciously aware of all aspects of being. Body, mind, spiritual balance. In the outer world experience, that will be expressed in a peacefulness for humanity.

Ancient prophesies, such as the Mayan, have predicted that year as being the end of one cycle, and the beginning of a new.

There is that which would be many indigenous cultures speaking to this transformational period of time in different ways of speaking, yet the essence is the same for the transmissions and transmutations of consciousness into a wholeness of being that allows for a peacefulness within the world of humankind.

And other indigenous groups such as the Hopi prophesies?

Here, too, is some accuracy in the sense of the essence of what is to come in the sense of common unity. There is a correctness, and when one looks out into the world of all this prophecy, or expressions of what is to come, have been much in alignment in its purest form. So there is a comfortableness within the beings that this can be true for when there are many varied sources of information that are collective such as this in thought and an agreement, one not privy to the other in their statement, then one can ascertain that this is truth.

How accurate are the biblical prophesies regarding this time we are moving into?

Their accuracy is in the purest of form or essence, however, note that there had been this information placed forward and then the documentation and then the translations, all done by humans with their own projections of their own beliefs and fears. So there have been, in the biblical expressions, much fear. For many beings of the past feared change, as many do now. However, having the experience of rapid change within the structure of the world, as there has been in the most recent hundred years, there is a greater comfortableness that evolves now with change and expansion and movement, as there was less opportunity for awareness, less opportunity for recognition of change prior to that. Humans were limited to contact one unto the other. Now with the global community, there is less fear of change because of that communication.

Is there more trust?

Awareness. It is this consciousness evolution that is quite profound for the earth in this time. Before there was not the connectedness and the awareness in the mind and the abilities addressed for the human experience. The inner strengths and knowings of humanity are in greater acceptance. And the experiences of the human, in that which would be multidimensional, will create less fear and more strength.

We have heard you say that we're living now in a time unlike any other in history energetically. Does that include two thousand years ago, or is it very similar energetically as it was then?

Energy about the world that has been astrologically aligned, that affects the world, is similar to that time. Yes. Know that energy cycles, and there are particular alignments that happen within the solar system, within the universe, that do affect one another. It is not only the effect to the earth, but the earth affects other planets and so forth. So it is to recognize that this alignment is happening now that happened in that time—the receptivity of this energy and the shift and changes for the human experience and for the world that humanity was not prepared fully for then, as they are now, on a vibrational frequency of the physical structure. Evolutionarily speaking.

It has been said that we now have a choice whether to move into this higher spiritual state, or to perceive as we currently do, or even to return to a more indigenous lifestyle. Is there any truth to this, or is it all really our own creation anyway?

It is a creation and it is a choice, yes, to go forward and to expand and to become more, consciously, or to remain the same. But in the remaining of the same, an uncomfortableness, for the frequency or the vibration will be so high that it will be uncomfortable to remain in the old way.

Speak more to that, please.

It would be physically uncomfortable, mentally uncomfortable to remain in the like manners of the past and not to adhere. Know that all beings are affected by the energy. And those that accept it and flow with it and are open to it have greater ease. Those that remain structured and resistant will be more agitated. And that agitation permeates the life experience, the body. Physically it can create an imbalance, an illness. So it is best taken to account, to open the self, to embrace the opportunity, and to move into the new millennium with the acceptance.

So we'll go forward in a higher, more spiritual state, then beyond that thousand years?

Correct. Expansion, awareness, acceptance. The ability to transform. All humanity will have the abilities of multidimensional experiences, not limited only to the earth, not limited only to this physical form. So when one becomes fully aware of their capabilities and the acceptance of one's divinity and perfection, that is, the expansion that happens is rapid. One cannot perceive in the conscious mind now what is to come. There are great blessings.

What role do you see technology playing in the new millennium?

There will be great technologies utilized in the new millennium, as it were, for there are great minds, and as the mind becomes stronger and there is greater awareness, more will be created. For beings will then see the unlimitness to the mind. So there would be great things changed, advanced upon, but more important, what one sees is the innate capabilities of humankind to love. That is the greatest change of all, is it not?

Is it possible that spirituality and technology actually merge at some point? We can, for instance, communicate telepathically, and technology seems to be moving into a place of near telepathic communication.

The tools will be made better by the experiences of the human, and the creativity of the human expanding then will be utilized to create tools, to create life experiences more refined. The creative aspect of humanity will flourish and therein the quality of life will be better.

What will the global political climate be like? You've spoken of a global community or common unity.

There would be a structure in places, a global political structure such as that which is your United Nations, and will be however, a bit more effective, and it is moving into that now. It would be representation from all countries that come about from meeting, for collaboration, for the betterment of humankind not for the separation of each other. The sciences and the arts bring about a global communication and sharing of great minds and great experiences and expressions that brings about a common dialogue, community, out of this creativity, and the assistance of one unto the other to make the quality of life better for all. A higher intent, is it not? The sciences bring about new technologies and new healing modalities that allows humanity to come into a greater fulfillment and healthful state and a timelessness; globally touching all countries, not only in those that have fine arts, but those that have natural resources, coming into balance and acceptance of caring for the earth together for the sustenance of humanity on all levels.

What role do you see organized religion playing in the future and what will the relationship be between the church and the global community?

What will be seen is changes within the environment of the religious communities and the churches that have been rigid in their structure, accommodating humanity in their own personal experience of spirit, for that will be how they would remain a factor. For beings, upon having their own personal experience of spirit and God, as it were, would seek out and understand the one God experientially, and seek out a structure that is comfortable for them in the sense of religion, or church, that supports their experience. So it becomes one church, ultimately, in the meaning of one belief in one God. How that is expressed in each individual will be important. There would be a non judgment of one another, an acceptance of cultures, an acceptance of beliefs and experiences, not to be thought of as separative, but to be learned from, and experienced from.

Will we see the end of communism sometime in the near future?

There would be that as there is a common unity that comes about for the betterment of humankind. There would not be the separateness in the political forms that have been. For it is not the politicians that make this change, it is the people within themselves. In doing so within themselves, express that externally and require it upon their state.

When are we going to see the demise of dictators?

As there is strength within humanity, there are strengths amongst peoples. There would not be allowed the personality to be in such power in a negative sense. There would be less fear. There will be empowerment. As there has been historically in the past, many hundreds of years passed there were kings, queens, hierarchy such as these that dictated to the peoples, did they not, about the land.

And there were different classes of people that were controlled by these personalities. It is not unlike what is happening today in those particular environments of dictatorship. However, as beings evolved consciously, those forms dissolved, did they not? So shall these.

Environmentally, how are we going to get our planet cleaned up?

As beings are more conscious and aware of their totality, they become more conscious and aware of their environment, for there is a recognition of the connectedness. So that is all a part of the whole.

Is the shift under way right now?

Yes.

So we are making a difference environmentally?

Yes.

Is global warming going to be a problem in the future?

There is a recognition of it and there is the consciousness to change it and shift it and that will come about, educationally speaking, for the masses.

How about our climate? Much has been much said regarding shifting of the poles, and earthquakes, and volcanic eruptions, and so forth.

There will not be a dramatic shift of the polarity of the planet. However, there is a recognition as ones become more aware of their environment, and the necessity of maintaining that which would be for the highest good of all. There need not be a concern of the melting of the poles. As to volcanic activity, and as to that which is earthquake activity that is natural to the earth. And that will continue. It is part of the organic workings of your earth planet.

What improvements do you see in the educational system going into the new millennium?

There will be an environment for creativity that heretofore has been limited. There will be a recognition of the technological abilities that will be utilized for this global conversation and education. There would be that which most importantly will be the works of the esteem of the student, bringing forth not only that which is the intellect, but the heart.

It has been absent in our teaching.

It has been. It has been most focused upon the intelligence and the intellect, but not that which is the heart and the integration of wholeness of the being. And there will be more attention paid to this.

Will this be a process that will take place in the home as well as in the schools?

Yes.

So there will be a shift in teaching consciousness?

Yes. But there is not much to be said. It is very simplistic. There would be the support of the young to evolve into the wholeness of their being from their hearts. There has been much emphasis upon the intellect and not enough upon the soul. And we are not speaking of religion. We are speaking of the wholeness of the individual. The acceptance of the self as a unique, perfect being, and as this evolves in humanity, it will be expressed in all areas of experience.

Is there going to be a problem with overpopulation in the future?

That is a probability, yes. But as beings become more conscious, and conscious of the environment, they are more conscious of procreation.

At some point there is a limit as to how many people can live on this planet in harmony. Are we reaching that point right now?

There is a reaching of the point, yes. But it has not been reached as yet.

What is the timing for a visitation or substantiation of life on other planets?

That has already begun.

Are we going to see in our lifetime communication or contact with beings from other planets?

Yes.

Will it coincide with the major shift to take place around 2012?

It would coincide. There would be information that there is this, and has been, ongoing interaction.

So our government and scientists have already begun this process?

Yes.

It now, then, becomes simply a matter of sharing it with the masses?

Correct.

Can you speak any more to that now?

No.

What more do you have to speak to regarding the new millennium?

Not to be caught up in what is to come, for that is of interest, but it is not affecting one's present experience in the moment. It is our desire and our teaching to draw beings into their momentary experience, to be fully who they are. And in doing such, will be drawn into the new millennium as whole beings expressing love of self, and love of neighbor as the self, as was taught two thousand years past. For it is a time of that. Many continue to live in the future or the past, and not live their life fully. Those moments are lost, so to speak. And living the life to the fullest extent and expressing the soulfulness of the self fully upon the planet allows for that which would be the peace that we have spoken about. Live that now. Engage in those opportunities now, within the self. And the fulfillment that one seeks in the millennium will be achieved.

How do you see our planet today?

Becoming aware. Through your ability to communicate globally there is an awareness and education that is occurring about the peoples of the world, the similarities and of course the diversity. Not divisiveness but diversity in expression in lifestyles and celebration of God. So when there is this knowledge and education of one another there is a lessening of judgment and hate. And there is a lessening of fear and an assistance to one another. For you are all connected. And through this ability to know in a global way it brings a community or a common unity amongst humankind.

Some people would see that as a bit of a stretch right now with some of the things going on in our world. Many people have asked about the war in Iraq and how we can most effectively disengage, remove ourselves from the struggle that's going on now. How do you see that?

Get out. Iraq would be in chaos, it is in chaos now. And there is an arrogance of thinking that these peoples could not speak to one another, or to engage so that there can be different states. There are three distinct communities that should each be allowed to govern. And then to have their common governorship and each voice be heard. It can be done. This has been a place of chaos and judgment of one another, so education is important.

How do you see the United States repairing our reputation internationally following this rather disappointing event in history?

We have said in the past it is not the politicians that bring peace; it is the arts and sciences that allow a dialogue amongst humankind for the betterment of all. And there will be a global economic structure as well, necessarily so, so that there is not the manipulations of the few to control the mass. So what occurs here is personalities of greater vision and greater communication and empowerment of a global entity much like your United Nations, but having greater influence, which it can—by being empowered. And this will come by the desire of the people.

What do you observe looking at us spiritual beings having a human experience, what is your observation of us?

We have great love for you. All of you. We see your struggles and it is about not seeking outwardly, not being forceful outwardly trying to change another's mind, but changing your own. Doing the soulful work of soul integration individually. Addressing the terrorist within, the lack of esteem and lack of self-love. For if all beings could address those issues within, there would be peace. For the acting out that you see, the wars, the imbalances are about the issues inside of the individuals being projected out. Easier said than done, is it not?

Many more are awakening to what we are talking about today. Many people have referred to it as many things of course. You know the shift of the ages, the great awakening and so forth. And you, since the mid-seventies, have spoken very clearly about life in the fifth dimension, the year 2012, the process of enlightenment called soul integration. I wanted to ask you to talk about the year 2012. A lot of people have been asking about the Mayan calendar, the end of time as we know it, all of the different variations on that. Please tell us about 2012 and the significance of that and between now and then.

Many speak of the new age. There is nothing new about it. We find it quite interesting that there must be a title for all the changes. There is a historical necessity, yes? However, the year 2012 is significant. Not that there would be a dramatic upheaval. But this has been going on for many years, this awakening. It is a pinnacle point, you might say, of change, of awarenesses, of change of procedures, of global economic community coming forth. Of this community awareness that is global conferences that will be available through your media and your computers and your tools, should we say? This awareness of one another, this comes about to create the global community of which we speak. And with a global economic structure in place there can be abundance for all. And knowing that they are diverse, human's diversity; it is a beautiful tapestry of your planet, of your Earth, of your human race. We see it as a beautiful thing that is occurring. Even though there is strife in that. When there is an imbalance in a physical body, that you call illness, does it not have to appear to be worse before better? In many circumstances it does, the fever gets very high before it breaks and then the body is better and cleansed. So that is what is similar to what is occurring to the human experience now.

In looking at the Mayan calendar, what is the significance of December 21, 2012, and what happens beyond that date?

That's what we've been speaking about. But it is important not to hold mind in thought of time. Humanity is so stuck on time—when this, when that. Perfect timing is what one should think, perfect soul's timing. So if you are fully present moment to moment in one's experience one lives the life to its fullest extent. For if you are projected too far into that future or what is going to be and what is not. Not that you should not make plans, but what we are saying is you make your plans or you have your intuition of what is to come or your desire, then you live into it. And the opportunities present themselves for that to occur, as you have made your mind-set for the creation is the thought. We have given you some thought about what is to come, but we prefer to not be so finite to date, then the human mind becomes fixated and not attentive to what is.

So in this being in the moment, this presence, what can you share with us about how to remain in this present moment?

It is not that you should not review your life, but stay not stuck in the past. Recognize the gifts, the circumstances that allowed you to grow. Not to hold on to them steadfastly so that you cannot move from them, but to recognize this was then and here I am now. Look what has happened in between and how I observe my life presently. So you have those moments of reflection necessarily so and you have moments of futuristic thinking—preferably not fearful thinking. But if you are too caught up in the past, oftentimes there is anger and upset, draw the self back to what is happening in the moment. If you are eating an apple, how does it taste, what is its texture? If you are speaking to someone, listen fully to what they are saying. If you are listening to music, hear every note. If you are too much in the future, and oftentimes may think in terms of fear (what if this were to happen or that), draw the self back to the moment again. If you are walking, be deliberate in your steps, feel the ground under your feet, feel your foot in the shoe, feel what is being experienced of the body in that moment, to draw yourself back to presence. So it is to be fully present in all action that you are doing, moment to moment and embrace it.

✤ *Reflections on The Future*

The significance of the year 2012
- Beginning of a thousand years of peace
- Brings forth a true global community (common unity)
- The formation of a global economic structure
- Marks the end of one cycle and the beginning of another
- A time prophesied by many indigenous groups

The accuracy of the biblical prophecies
- Accurate in their essence
- Influenced by the projections of the fears and beliefs of human beings who participated in their transcription
- Written for the consciousness of humanity two thousand years ago
- Humanity is more evolved, less fearful than two thousand years ago

Similarities energetically between now and two thousand years ago
- Astrological alignments very similar
- An energy of change and evolution present in both times
- Humanity is more prepared now than then.

The choice to remain in the old ways or to go forward into the new
- Will be agitating and uncomfortable to remain stuck in old patternings
- Frequency and vibration for change is going to be too high to ignore.
- Greater disease for those who do not embrace the growth opportunities
- Choosing growth will result in greater fulfillment.

Beyond the year 2012

- No reversal of evolution
- Humanity recognizes the abilities to have multidimensional experiences
- Human beings not limited to the physical body
- The conscious mind not yet able to perceive what is to come

The role of technology in the new millennium
- Great technological expansion
- Creativity of humanity to flourish; innate capabilities of human beings to be the greatest advancement

Global political climate
- Establishment of global political structure like the U.N., but more effective
- Sciences and the arts create greater global communication.
- Collaboration for the betterment of humankind, not separation
- A coming into balance and acceptance for the caring of the earth
- New technologies and healing modalities to be shared with all of humanity for greater fulfillment and health

The role of organized religion in the new millennium
- Will encourage direct personal experience of God
- Less rigidity in their structure
- Nonjudgment of one another
- Acceptance of beliefs and experiences of other cultures

The end of communism and dictatorships
- Brought about by the change that takes place within each person
- No longer be the separateness in the political forms
- Less fear and more empowerment
- Old patternings fall away.

Environment and climate
- Greater consciousness and awareness
- Human beings taking more personal responsibility
- Greater education
- No dramatic shift of the polarity of the planet
- Earth will continue to cleanse itself.

The future of education
- Greater environment for creativity
- Continued development of technological abilities
- Much greater emphasis on the self-esteem of the student
- Concentration on the heart and the integration of the wholeness of the student
- More emphasis will be placed on the whole being.

Interaction with extraterrestrials
- Has already begun
- Governments and scientists are already involved.
- Mass recognition of contact will coincide with the year 2012.

Epilogue

As you have read this dialogue, you've heard the process of multidimensional soul integration as the common thread woven through every chapter. We can share with you from our personal experiences that this process works. You simply have to make the choice to begin. There are no mistakes, and by simply placing the intent and practicing meditation daily, you will begin to open to your full soul.

The process truly does expand your powers of perception and will lead you to a place of self-empowerment, profound experiences, and peak performance in all aspects of your life. And it does open you up to miracles. It's an ongoing, unfolding process occurring in the most magnificent time in the history of this planet. We are very excited for you as you continue on your own journey of self-discovery. And we ask you to share with us your experiences as your consciousness expands.

This new book of THEO's wisdom reflects our desire to introduce you to their insights on many topics. It is our intent in subsequent books and CDs to explore these topics, and many more, on a much deeper level. As THEO has often stated, "In the asking, it will be given." The depth and content of these future projects is limited only by the curiosity, imagination, and intellect of humanity, as this source of wisdom is unlimited.

Index

Acknowledgments

To our parents, Dorothy Williams, and Jere and Alicia Gillette, for their unconditional loving support. To our children, Stephanie, Jeff, Cathy, and Jennifer, thank you for choosing us as your parents and for being our inspiration. We thank all the students of THEO's teachings from around the world, who have shared their life questions with us so that this book could be written. And last but not least, we would like to express our gratitude to our literary agents, Kristina Holmes and Michael Ebeling, for their encouragement and commitment to sharing THEO's teachings with a global audience.

About the Authors

In 1969, **Sheila Gillette** nearly died from a pulmonary embolism suffered after the birth of her third child. In the months that followed this near-death incident, she started to experience various types of psychic phenomenon and soon began trance channeling—first, a nonphysical entity by the name of Orlos and then a consortium of twelve archangels collectively known as **THEO**.

THEO began speaking through her in 1975, and since that time, Sheila has been astonishing radio, television, and live audiences throughout the United States and Europe as the direct voice-channel for THEO. Since 1997, Sheila's husband, **Marcus Gillette,** has partnered with Sheila in moderating/facilitating AskTHEO Live gatherings throughout the United States. Together, they host the multimedia website AskTHEO.com. They have also spoken before several businesses, communities, and nonprofit organizations and currently offer workshops around the nation.

If you would like to know more about their work with THEO please visit www.asktheo.com. To inquire about booking Sheila, Marcus and Theo for TV, Radio, or live events please email them at theo@asktheo.com or call 720-344-2932.

Made in the USA
Las Vegas, NV
09 March 2023